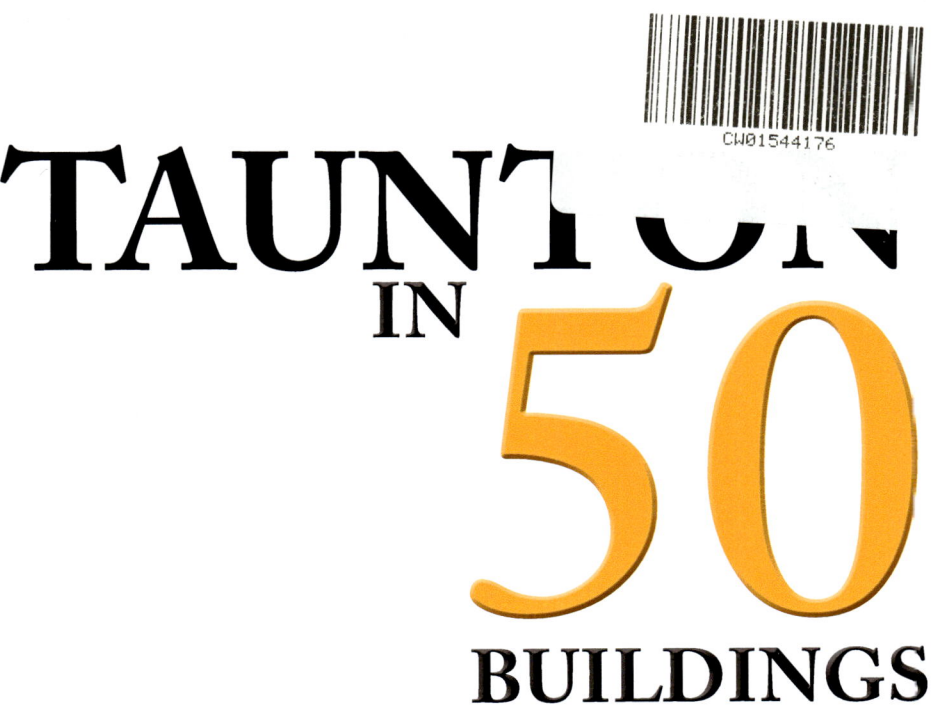

TAUNTON IN 50 BUILDINGS

LYNNE CLEAVER

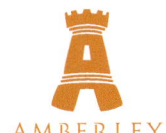

To my late mother, who didn't get to see this one finished.
Gillian (Gill) Ruth Boulter, 1935–2023

First published 2024

Amberley Publishing, The Hill, Stroud
Gloucestershire GL5 4EP

www.amberley-books.com

Copyright © Lynne Cleaver, 2024

The right of Lynne Cleaver to be identified as the Author of this work has been asserted in accordance with the Copyrights, Designs and Patents Act 1988.

Map contains Ordnance Survey data © Crown copyright and database right [2024]

All rights reserved. No part of this book may be reprinted or reproduced or utilised in any form or by any electronic, mechanical or other means, now known or hereafter invented, including photocopying and recording, or in any information storage or retrieval system, without the permission in writing from the Publishers.

British Library Cataloguing in Publication Data.
A catalogue record for this book is available from the British Library.

ISBN 978 1 3981 1678 8 (print)
ISBN 978 1 3981 1679 5 (ebook)

Typesetting by SJmagic DESIGN SERVICES, India.
Printed in Great Britain.

Contents

Map	4
Key	6
Introduction	7
The 50 Buildings	9
Bibliography	95
Acknowledgements	96

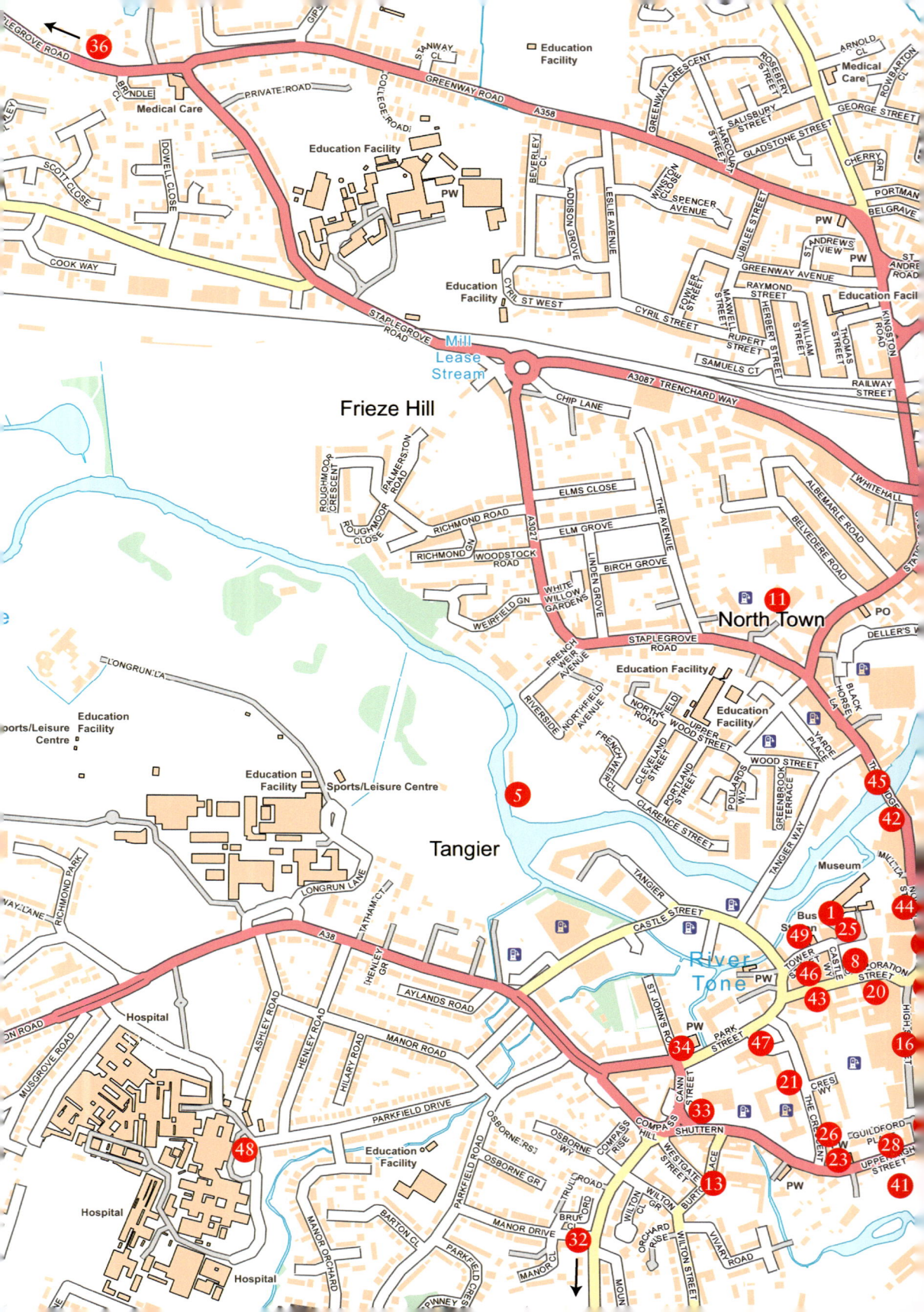

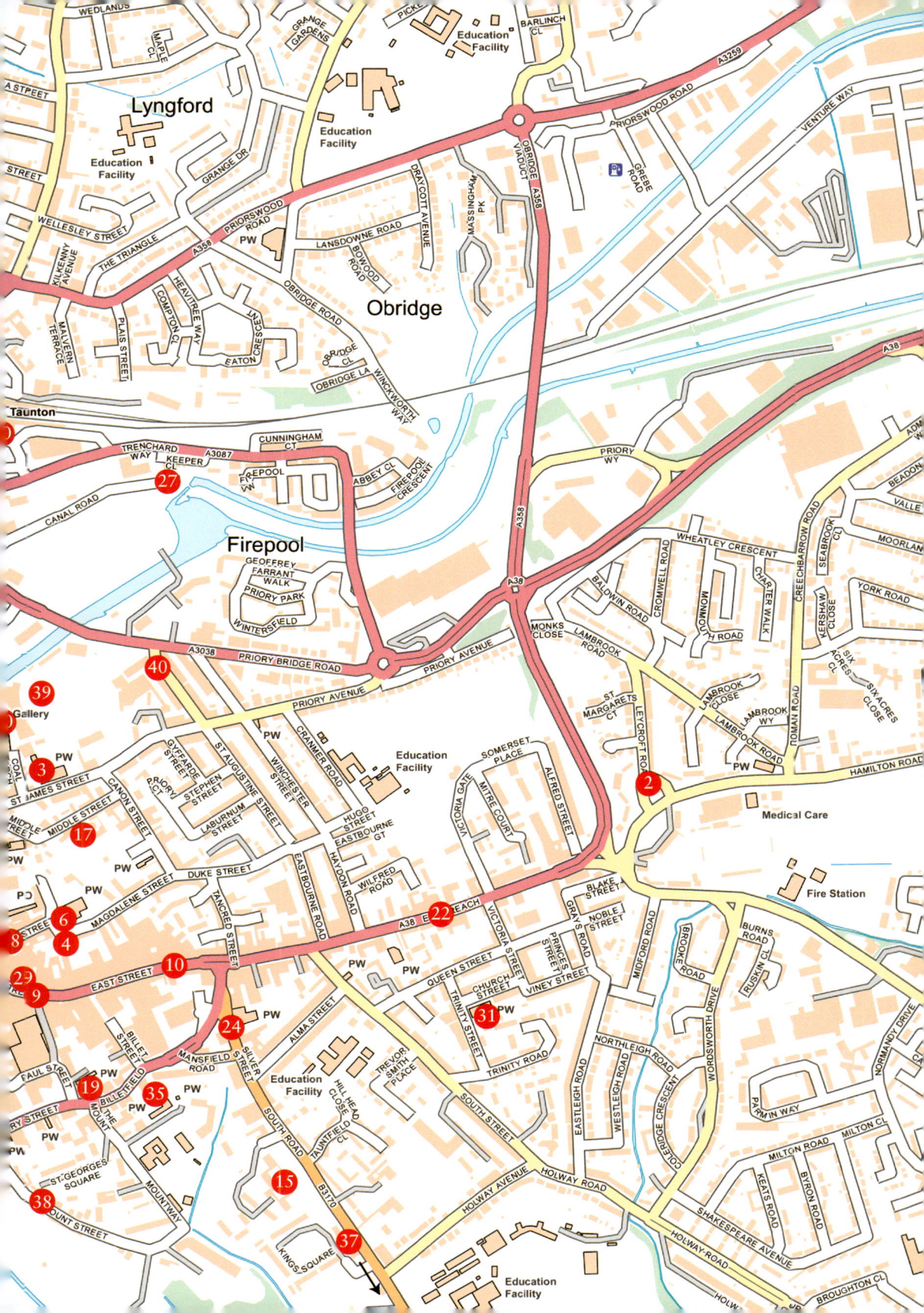

Key

1. Taunton Castle, *c.* 1100
2. St Margaret's Hospital, *c.* 1174
3. St James' Church, Twelfth Century
4. Taunton Minster (formerly St Mary Magdalene), Twelfth Century
5. French Weir, River Tone, Thirteenth Century
6. St Mary's Vicarage, 1308
7. Tudor House, No. 15 Fore Street, Fourteenth Century
8. Municipal Buildings, 1522
9. Waterstones (formerly The County Hotel), Sixteenth Century
10. Gray's Almshouses, 1635
11. Flook House, Seventeenth Century
12. Unitarian Chapel, 1721
13. Wilton Gaol (later Taunton Gaol), 1754
14. Market House, 1770s
15. Franciscan Convent, 1772
16. Hatcher & Sons, 1775
17. Octagon Chapel, 1776
18. Hammet Street, 1788
19. United Reformed Church, 1797
20. Bath Place
21. The Crescent, 1807
22. Taunton and Somerset Hospital, East Reach, 1810
23. The Temple, 1812
24. Silver Street Baptist Church, 1815
25. Castle Hotel, 1816
26. St George's Chapel (then Masonic Hall), 1821
27. Firepool Lock, 1823
28. West Somerset Savings Bank, 1831
29. Cheapside, 1835
30. Railway Station, 1842
31. Holy Trinity Church, 1842
32. Queen's College, 1847
33. Shire Hall, 1855
34. St John the Evangelist Church, 1858
35. Roman Catholic Church of St George, 1860
36. Taunton School, 1867
37. King's College, 1867
38. The Keep, Jellalabad Barracks, 1880
39. County Ground, 1882
40. Collar Factory, 1888
41. Vivary Park, 1893
42. Tone Bridge, 1895
43. School of Art, 1905
44. Post Office, 1911
45. Deller's Café, 1923
46. Gaumont Palace, 1932
47. County Hall, 1935
48. Musgrove Park Hospital, 1942
49. Bus Station, 1952
50. Brewhouse Theatre, 1977

Introduction

Taunton was well established by the time of the Domesday Book in 1086. Early settlers were attracted by the fertile lands of the Tone Vale, and a crossing point over the River Tone gave rise to the foundation of the town. Archaeology has provided evidence of a Neolithic and Roman presence, although no specific building sites have been identified.

Taunton Castle dates to the eighth century, medieval churches were founded in the mid-seventh century and an Augustinian priory was in the vicinity of the Somerset County Cricket Ground. At the other end of the scale there is the newly created Hydrographic Office (2019) and the newly opened Coal Orchard Development (2022), situated between St James Quarter and the Brewhouse Theatre, and the Firepool area between the town and railway station both continue to be developed with modern housing and leisure facilities, adding to the long history of the town.

The 'Taunton Estate' belonged to Taunton Minster and lands were added during the eighth and ninth centuries. This estate was granted to the See of Winchester (the 'see' refers to the jurisdiction, or care of, the bishops of Winchester). The kings of Wessex retained the majority of the manor and they developed it into an important trading centre with markets and burgage plots. Burgages were lands and property held by townspeople in return for fixed rents. The town even had its own mint. By Domesday, the whole estate was under the control of the See of Winchester. Bishops William Gifford and Henry of Blois were influential in the development of the castle and religious buildings of the time.

The thirteenth century saw the development of one of the town's major industries – the cloth trade. By the twentieth century the town was famed for the production of shirts and shirt collars.

Taunton has had a Member of Parliament since the thirteenth century, and occasionally regional parliaments were held in the town. It is now Somerset's county town and responsible for administration of county-wide matters, working from County Hall.

Military skirmishes that have occurred here include the war of succession between Stephen and Matilda, the Wars of the Roses, Perkin Warbeck's rebellion against Henry VII, the Civil War (it supported the Parliamentarians) and the Monmouth Rebellion in 1685.

Transportation methods from turnpike roads and the river and canal to railways and finally the motorway infrastructure has led to land infill, resulting in a spread outwards particularly in the last two centuries, a process that is still ongoing with new housing estates popping up in vast numbers.

In this volume I hope to guide the reader through Taunton's history in an enlightening and enjoyable manner by looking at some of the town's buildings.

The 50 Buildings

1. Taunton Castle, c. 1100

It is believed that Taunton Castle was originally erected beside the River Tone as an ancient wooden defence by King Ine in the eighth century. Traces of an Anglo-Saxon burial ground have been identified on the site, which modern techniques have dated to the seventh century. Excavations in 1951/52 revealed part of the earliest building: a wide double-barrelled undercroft below the floor of the Great Hall, now the main hall of the museum.

In AD 904 the Bishop of Winchester bought the Taunton Estate from the Crown. Development and alterations made by Bishops William Gifford and Henry of Blois form the basis of the castle today (the keep and inner bailey).

The thirteenth-century castle had a ground-floor hall, bishop's chamber, salsary (a room for preparing sauces) and chapel (St Nicholas). Access to the outer ward was from the east gate (Castle Bow) with portcullis and drawbridge, the west gate

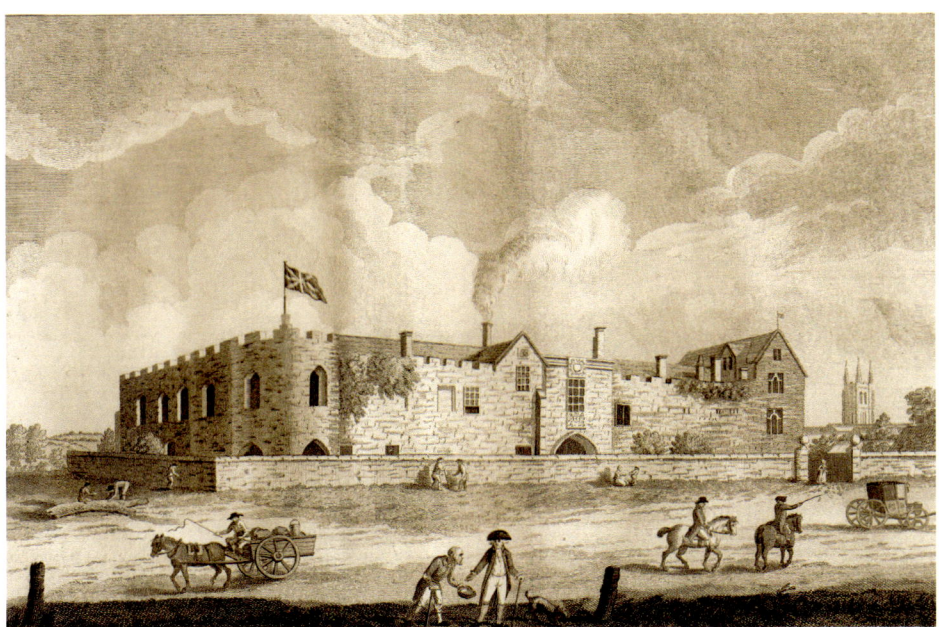

An engraving from 1790 showing Taunton Castle as it was then.

with drawbridge, or the water gate. In the outer ward there were barns, granaries, stables, a dairy, dovecote and chapel (St Peter). The inner castle (courtyard) had a further portcullis and drawbridge.

Although mainly an administrative centre for the manor of Taunton Estate rather than a military stronghold, the castle was not immune to the odd skirmish. Lord Bonville, a Lancastrian, besieged Thomas de Courtenay in 1451; Perkin Warbeck ('the Pretender') caused trouble in 1497; and the Civil War resulted in damage including the near destruction of Bishop Fox's schoolhouse.

Benjamin Hammet took over the lease and made major alterations, including division of some courtrooms, addition of the judges' lodgings and filling in the moat. Many original features were altered.

The Quarter Sessions and Assize Courts were held in the Great Hall until 1857. The most famous trial was the 'Bloody Assizes' following the Monmouth Rebellion, resulting in 526 prisoners being tried and many hung.

The records for Taunton Deane were held here until moved to Somerset Record Office in 1936. In 1874, Somerset Archaeological and Natural History Society bought the castle, saving it from destruction, and it now houses the county museum, which was leased to the County Council in 1958. The Military Museum was added in 1974.

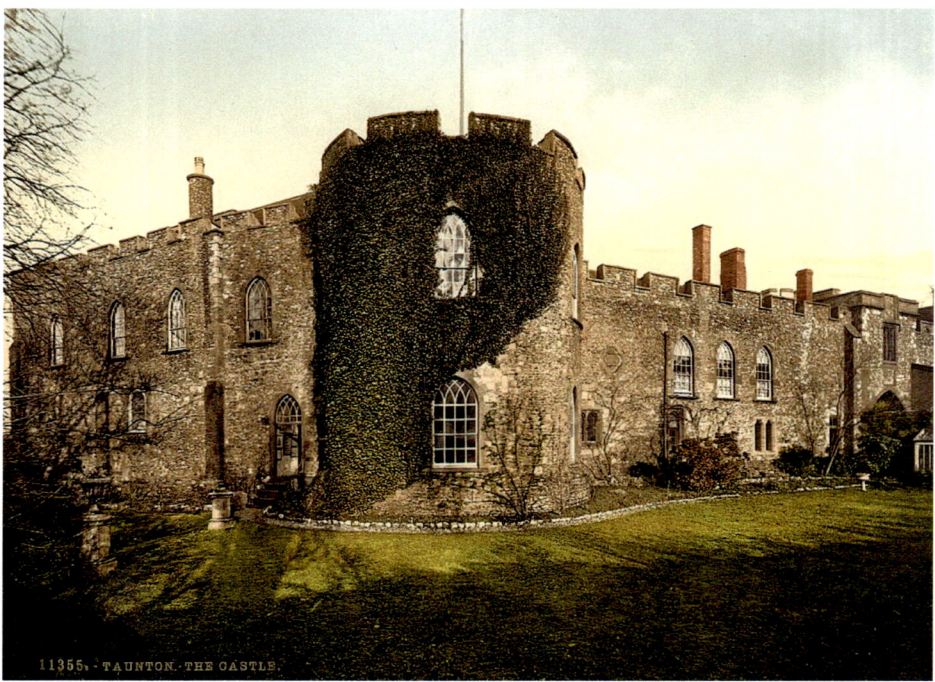

This postcard from around 1890 shows there has been little change, with the exception of a few more windows. (Courtesy of Detroit)

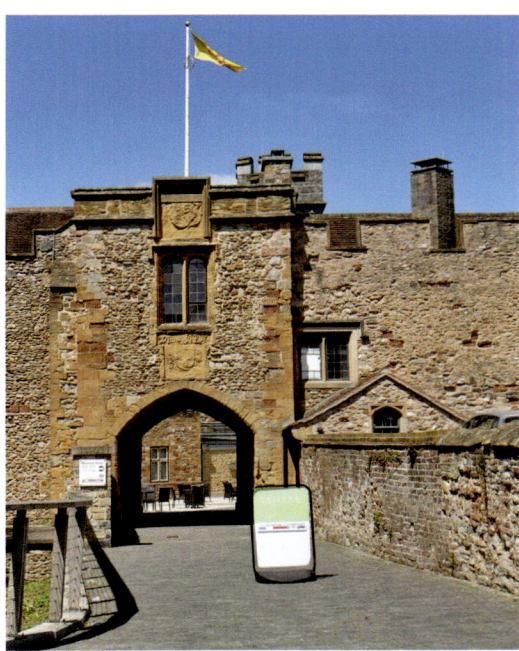

The archway into the inner courtyard, which is now an outside seating area for the café.

2. St Margaret's Hospital, c. 1174

St Margaret's Hospital is situated off Hamilton Road. Founded in 1174, the original hospital belonged to Taunton Priory. The buildings were destroyed by fire, and Abbot Richard Beere of Glastonbury was responsible for rebuilding in the late fifteenth and early sixteenth centuries. This is commemorated in a worn tablet to the front of the building displaying the initials 'R.B.' below an abbot's mitre.

The leprous brethren of St Margaret's without Taunton were granted royal protection in 1278 and were funded by charitable benefactors who left money to the 'spytelhouse' or 'lazar-house'. In 1612, the building was converted to almshouses but continued to house lepers until 1874. A chapel attached to the building was sold in 1549 and then demolished in 1930.

The accommodation provided each resident with a sitting room, fireplace and cooking facilities, and a small bedroom upstairs.

In 1936, Taunton Town Council proposed demolishing the building but a letter from the Somerset Rural Community Council (SRCC) published in the *Taunton Courier* pleaded with them to allow the Council for Protection of Rural England to view and come up with alternative suggestions for what they described as a 'unique relic of medieval design'. Thankfully, the SRCC took the building over and moved the residents to purpose-built accommodation in West Monkton. Internal alterations in 1939 by the Rural Community Council saw the eastern end opened to the roof whilst the other four rooms were altered and features removed. It was reported that during the reconditioning begun in January 1939

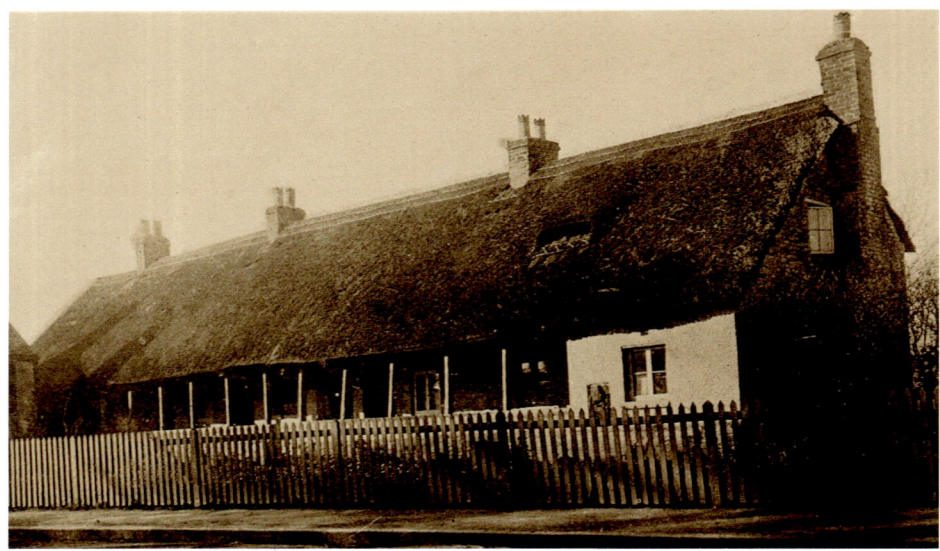

Above: St Margaret's Hospital, 1909 – the older date plaque can be seen to the right of the wooden pillars.

Below left: The 1939 restoration stone displaying the Somerset dragon.

Below right: One of the doorways into the cottages, complete with a thatched roof.

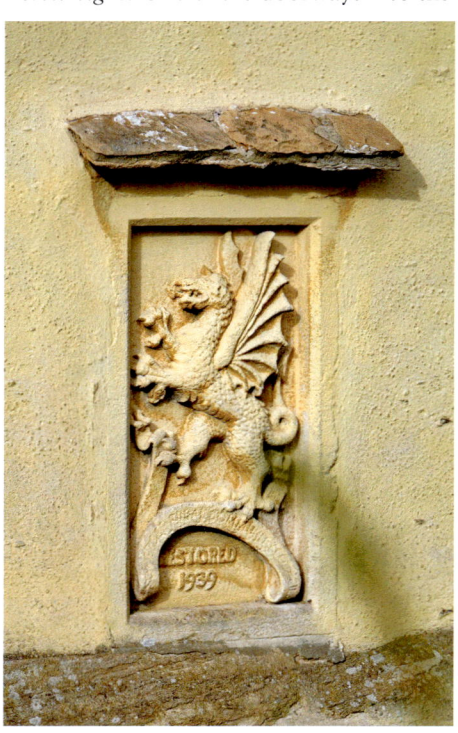
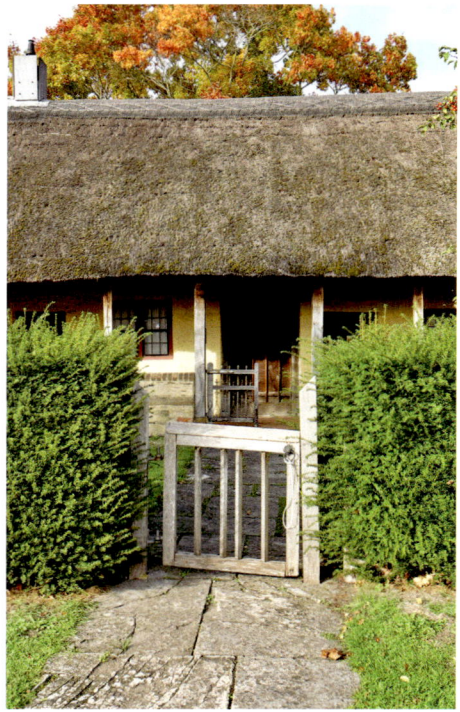

(Mr Mowbray A. Green, architect; Mr F. Bird, building supervisor; and works carried out by the Somerset Guild of Master Craftsmen), 'fine oak beams and a fireplace had been discovered'. The building was opened in July and a restoration stone was added to the west end of the frontage, matching that of the early restoration stone to the east end.

In 1958, Pevsner noted that the building had the original oak doorways and a thatched roof. He also stated that a 'semicircle of neo-Georgian council housing' had been built around the building. St Margaret's is now restored as housing.

3. St James' Church, Twelfth Century

St James' Church is situated in a medieval suburb of Taunton, outside the town defences. It was established in the twelfth century and was associated with the Augustinian priory also outside the town. It wasn't until 1539 that St James became a parish in its own right.

Alterations, improvements and repairs have left their own mark. Enlarged in the fifteenth and nineteenth centuries, the latter was almost a total rebuild under the instruction of Somerset architect Richard Carver. A gallery was added around 1836 which created an extra 300 seats. Just under fifty years later it was removed. The 120-foot tower was rebuilt in the 1870s from Sampford Brett red sandstone donated by Sir Alexander Acland Hood. The tower is topped with a weathervane, which has the following inscription on the cock's wings:

> A native am I and my name is Tom
> A jolly, gay bird, but I have no song
> I watch the wind, I keep events
> Which always have been my intents

The interior is spacious. Entry is through the tower, which has a fifteenth-century fan vault ceiling. A pulpit from 1633 crafted from oak with pattern of suns and mermaids was repaired and altered in 1884. The fifteenth-century font was also altered by addition of a thick base in the nineteenth century and was described by Pevsner as one of the most decorated in the county. It was reported in *The Builder* that two of the adorning figures were similar to two remaining in the tower and therefore it was estimated that the font was of the same age as the tower. There is much in the way of stained glass, mainly from the nineteenth century. However, one window from the 1950s depicts children and was donated by John and Jessie Spiller to celebrate that eleven nephews returned from the Second World War. The church font and children of the world are depicted and one of the quotes reads: 'Remember now thy creator in the days of thy youth.'

In 2001, a project to replace the floor uncovered some remains of the medieval building.

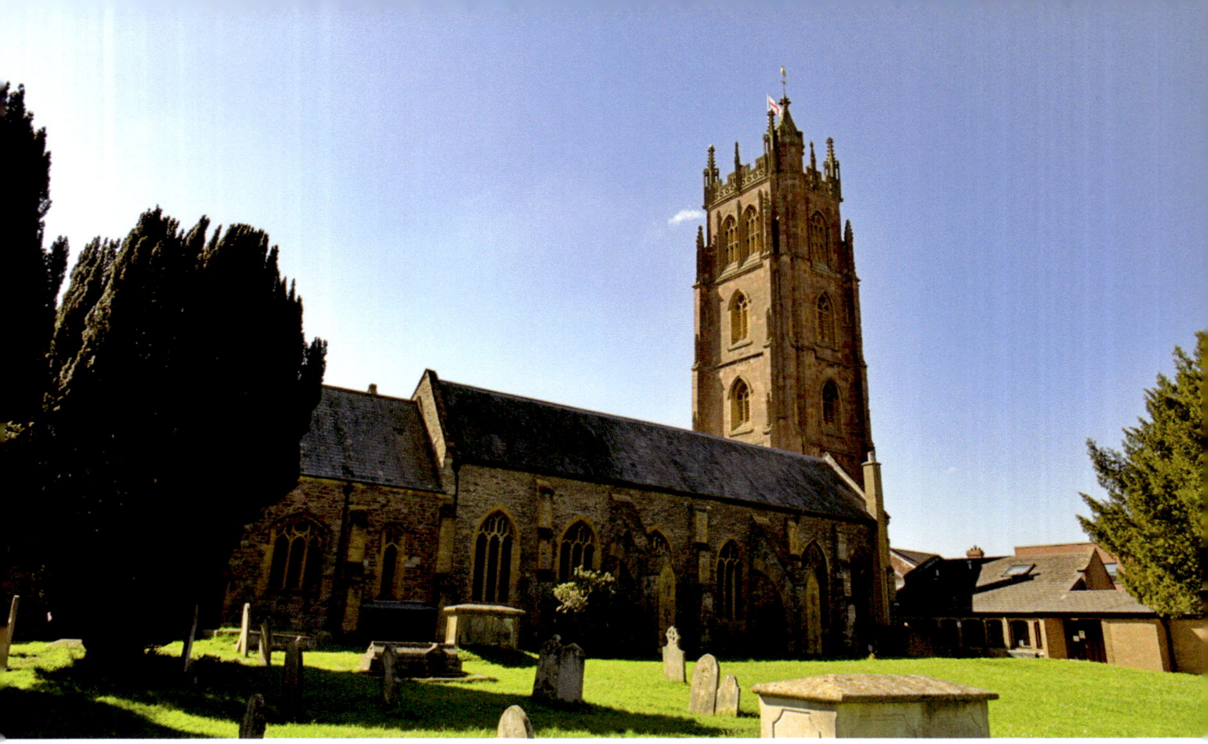

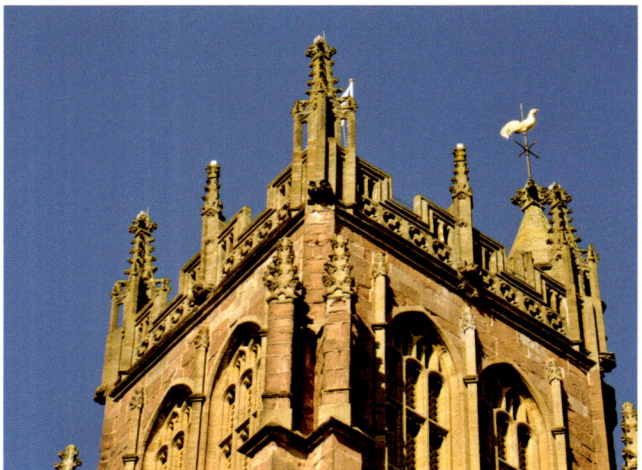

Above: St James' Church with the church offices to the right.

Left: The top of St James' Church tower, complete with weathervane.

4. Taunton Minster (formerly St Mary Magdalene), Twelfth Century

Taunton Minster building dates to the twelfth century, but the origins of the Christian community in Taunton go back much further. Sources differ, with some saying that Christianity was brought to Taunton by King Ine of the West Saxons during the eighth century and that he established a minster on the current site.

This stone church building was built by Henry of Blois during the twelfth century, and it served as a chapel of the priory. In 1308, it became a parish church – an event that was celebrated 700 years later in 2008 with the addition of beautiful glass doors designed and engraved by Tracey Sheppard FGE (Fellow of the Guild of Glass Engravers).

The original tower was built between 1488 and 1514, but by the mid-nineteenth century it had become unsafe so was rebuilt as an exact copy. A mid-Victorian author reported that the initials 'R. B.' could be seen on shields held by two angels on the upper belfry windows, and wondered if this referred to Richard Beere. A survey of the condition was undertaken in 1852 by Mr C. E. Giles who was suspended in mid-air by a basket using pulleys. It is 163 feet high and took four years to build, being completed in September 1862 by architect Sir Gilbert Scott.

The roof is Tudor and the porch has surviving sixteenth-century masonry. Some of the statues have been added and replaced throughout the history of the church.

As with many churches of this antiquity and size there is too much to do it justice in this small entry, so I will highlight just a few:

- The magnificent sixteenth-century ceiling painted with angels.
- The memorials to some of the town's benefactors, including Sir Robert Gray and Richard Huish.
- The Soldiers' Corner, a chapel dedicated to the Somerset Light Infantry.
- The War Memorial Cross in the churchyard, designed by West Country architect Frederick Bligh Bond and erected in 1920.
- The aforementioned glass doors.

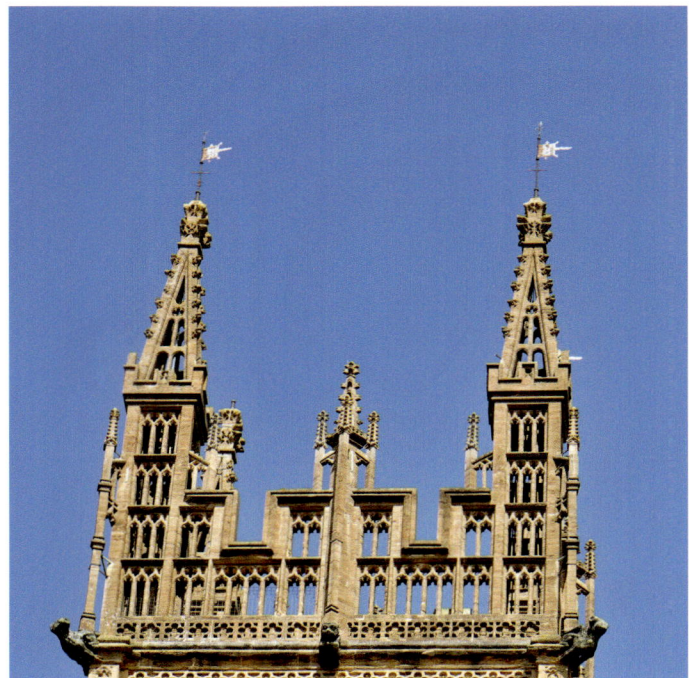

The crown of the tower pierced with two-storey arcading – tall pinnacles are at each corner.

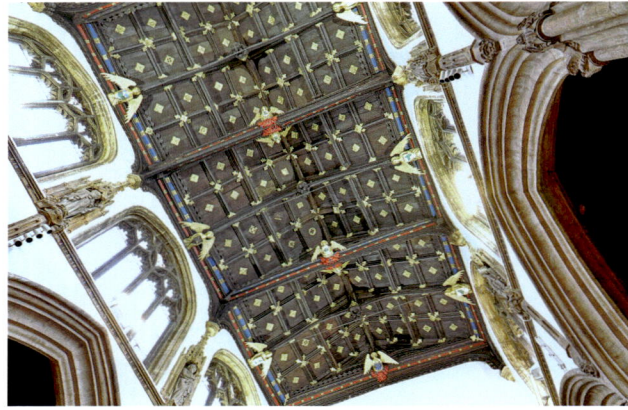

Left: The sixteenth-century ceiling was gilded in 1968.

Below: St Mary Magdalene Church, now Minster, as photographed in the 1890s. (Courtesy of Detroit)

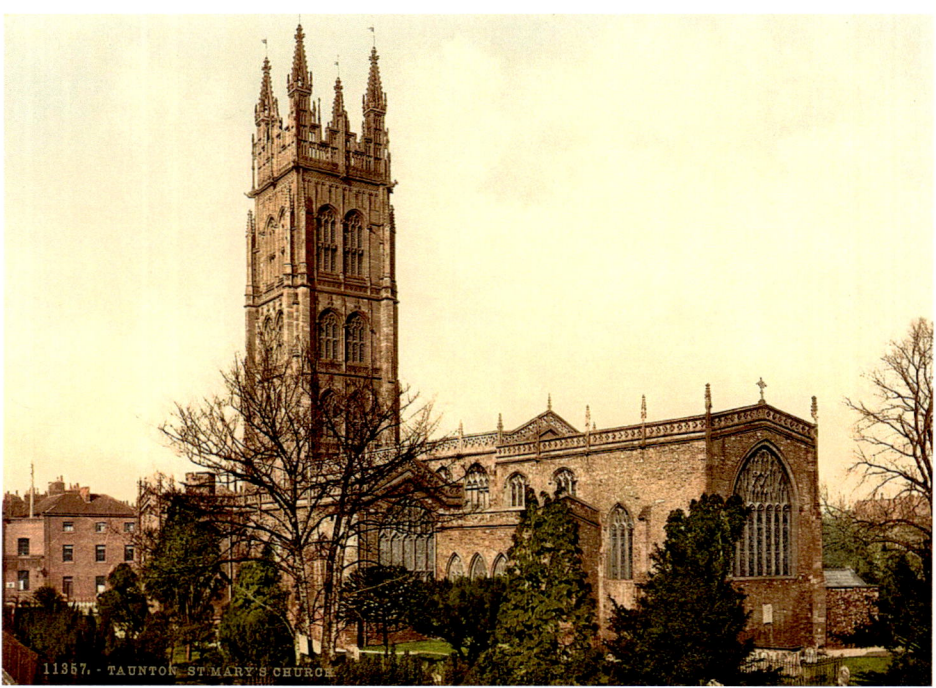

5. French Weir, River Tone, Thirteenth Century

French Weir has been a public park since about 1893 and was previously meadow. The River Tone snaked around the countryside here before heading into the centre of Taunton. Making use of the natural geography, the river's flow was diverted by the weir to power fulling and corn mills to the north of the castle by a newly built mill stream in what is now Goodland Gardens. The fulling mill was the earliest-recorded mill in the south-west of England, dating to the early thirteenth century. Fulling or tucking was part of the process of cloth manufacture and involved cleansing the woven fabric.

A sixteenth-century rebuild of the mill following flooding took place over three years and cost just over £100, which is recorded in the Bishop of Winchester's pipe rolls (these were the financial records of the English Exchequer and cover a period of 700 years). The area was prone to flooding; damage was caused in 1866 when the piers of a bridge were swept away, and again in 1910. The current weir was rebuilt in 1914/15.

A popular prank seemed to be to remove planks from one of the wooden bridges, potentially causing personal harm to anyone walking over in the dark. The *Taunton Courier* reported deaths caused by drowning – some accidental, some suicide. As a popular place for bathing, a need for privacy was identified by the Victorians and the construction of a safe and secluded place was debated. This resulted in a Bathing Station below the weir, with wooden changing cabins and a brick and concrete waterfront erected in 1862. The exterior was tarred and the interior whitewashed. An area was fenced off, seats and steps were constructed, as was a lodge for an attendant to enable private and safer bathing. Facilities could be enjoyed for an annual subscription of 2s 6d. In 1865, the first annual swimming and diving competition took place, with cups and medals being awarded.

This bathing station was replaced by a newer one above the weir in the 1920s which had diving boards, a water chute and grab chains for the swimmers to hold on to. Use of the bathing station waned as the water quality declined. However, it wasn't until 1930 that new undercover swimming baths in St James Street opened.

The twentieth-century weir, with salmon ladder and canoe portage to the right.

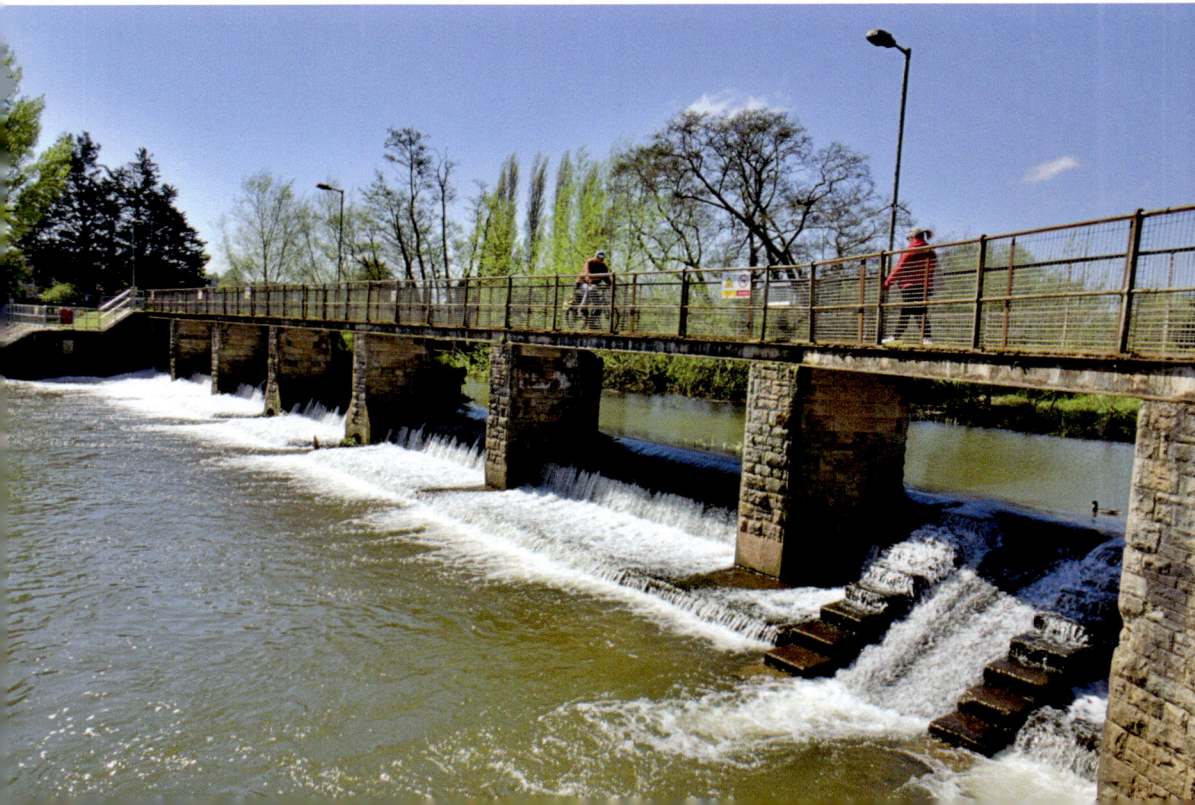

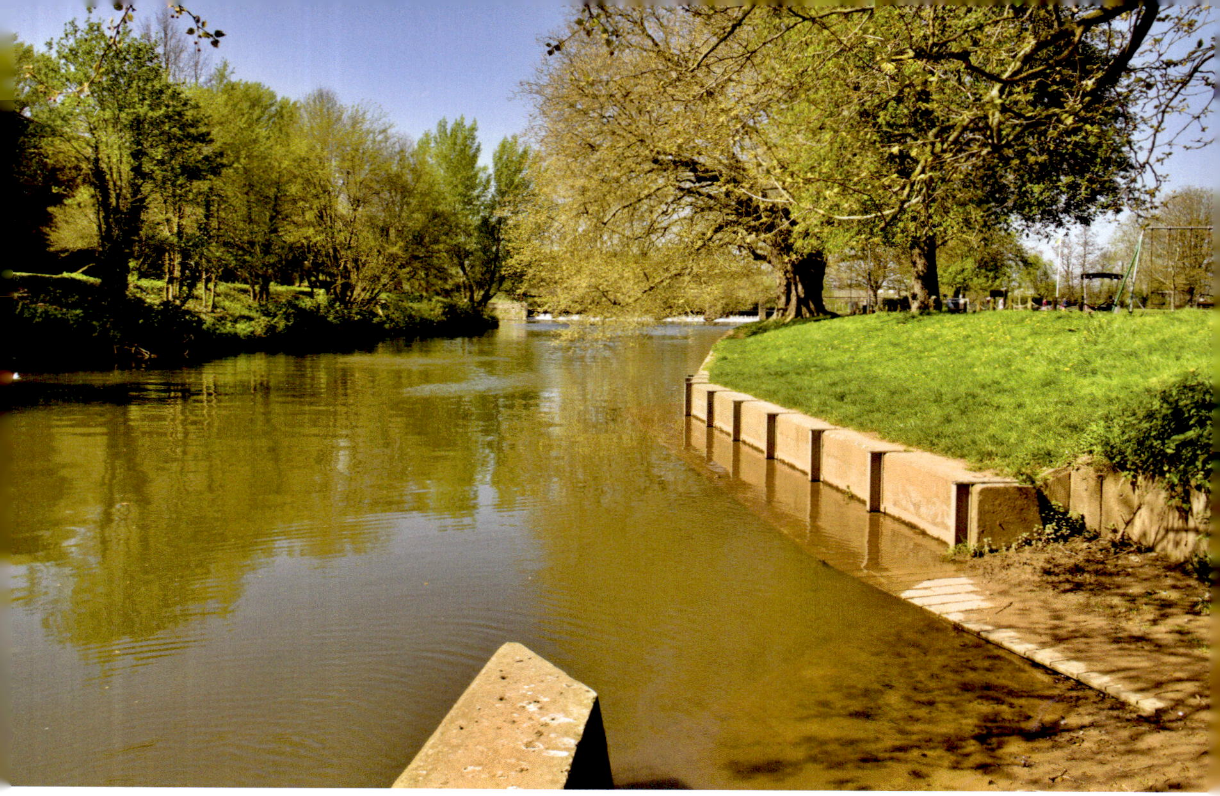

Above: The site of the first public bathing place on the River Tone at French Weir.

Below: Taunton Centre for Outdoor Activity and Community Hub is built on the site of the 1920s bathing station, with this section of river still used for 'wild' swimming.

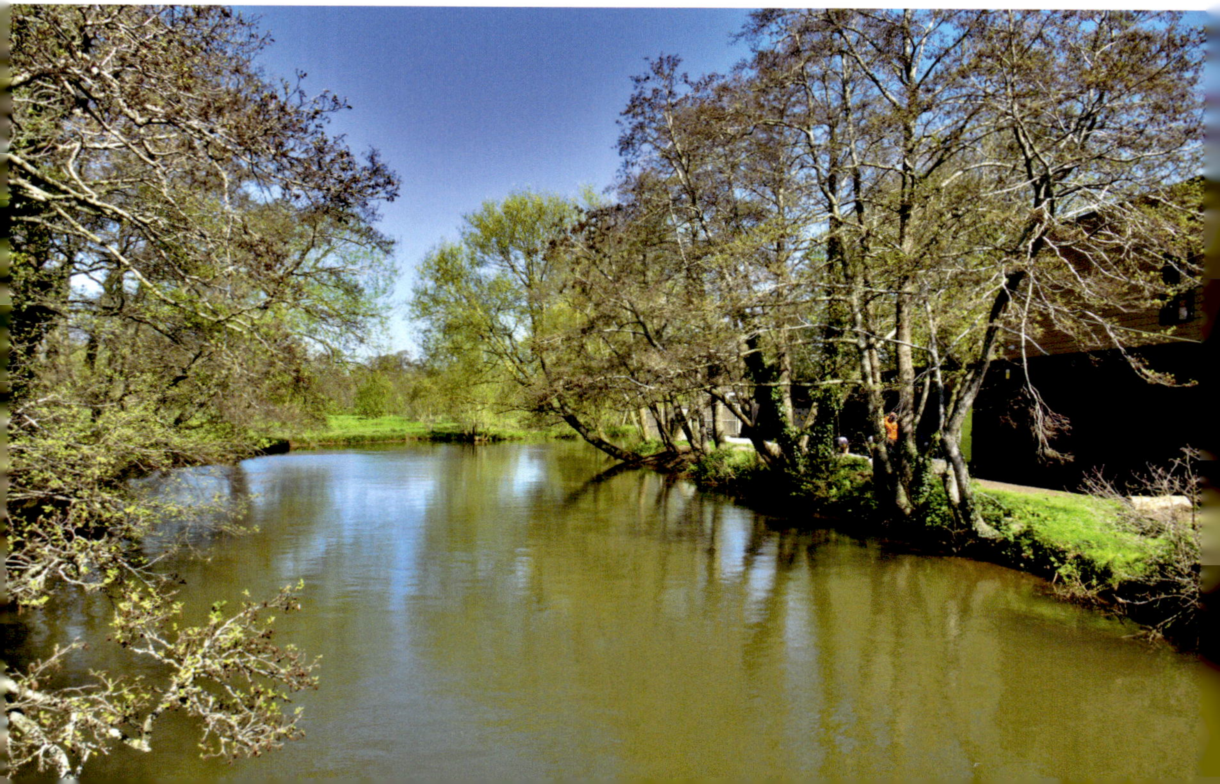

6. St Mary's Vicarage, 1308

St Mary's Vicarage falls within the medieval area of the town and is positioned north of Taunton Minster's churchyard. The earliest features in the current building are from the sixteenth and early seventeenth century, but the original building is thought to date to 1308. This is the year that St Mary's became a parish church rather than a chapel of the priory.

The house comprises two storeys, is built with red brick and has a tiled roof. The ground floor has mullioned windows, old oak door frames and a brick porch with a pointed stone arch to the centre.

In 1905, the Venerable William Henry Askwith, Archdeacon and Vicar of Taunton, was a virtual prisoner in his home as thirty-five-year-old Henry J. C. Reed, solicitor, was caught on several occasions causing damage to the property, roaming the grounds with a revolver and uttering obscenities. Reed was charged and imprisoned for two months, the Bench considering his behaviour more that of 'a madman than a sane person'.

In 2019, the seven-bedroom vicarage was sold by the church, with the selling agent stating that the house was in need of modernisation.

The vicarage is largely hidden from view, but glimpses offer a view of some of the decorative brickwork.

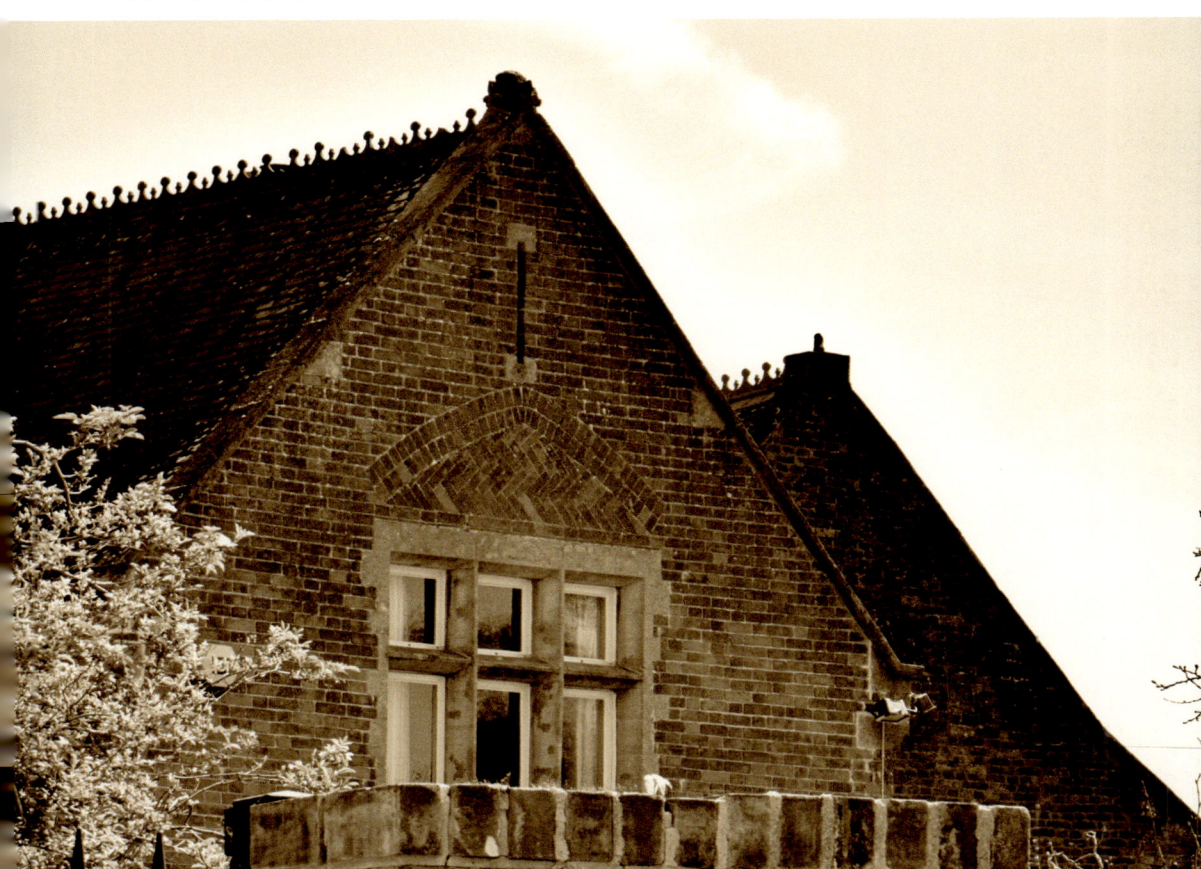

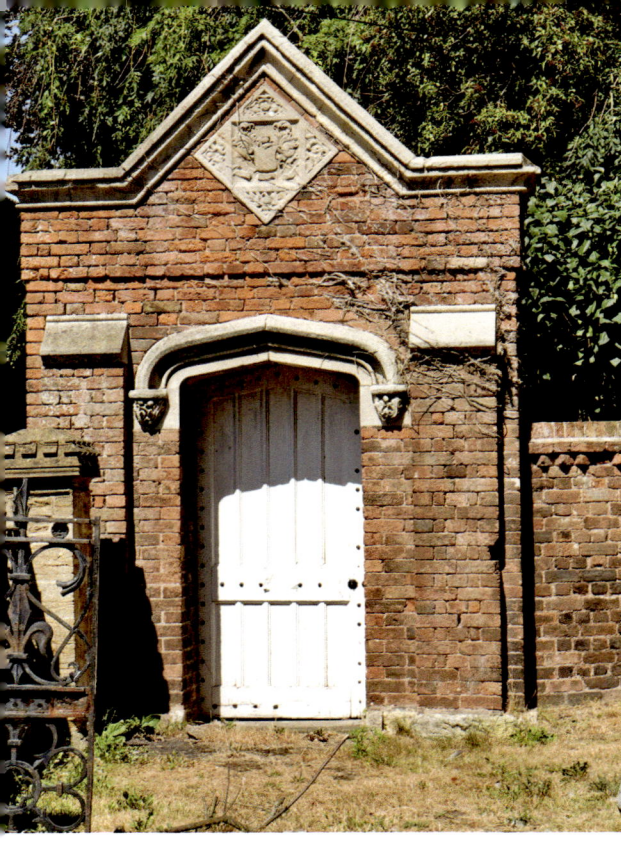

The gateway through to the vicarage garden has a four-centred arch, above which is a heraldic device.

7. Tudor House, No. 15 Fore Street, Fourteenth Century

Tudor House is the oldest-surviving domestic building in town. It is half-timbered and, using dendrochronology, its roof timbers have been dated to 1323/24. Inside the original construction, hand-sawn beams and features can be seen.

Records indicate that it was the home of the Marchaunt family up to the early fifteenth century, then passed to the Portman family who let it to wool merchant and clothier Thomas Trowbridge. He added the current façade, which brought the frontage forward by about 1.5 metres in 1578, the date recorded under a window with the initials 'T. T. & I. T.' (the latter is his wife Joan – the letters J and I were interchangeable at that time). Behind this façade is a late medieval hall with an open trussed roof.

To the rear is a courtyard which gives access to the Orchard Shopping Centre. A two-storey attached building probably housed servants to the main house.

More recent occupants have been a 'grocer, tea dealer and tallow chandler' business, which was run by the Turle family for three generations. The Turles took over an established business run by John Clitsome in the early nineteenth century and continued until sold in 1870. The business was run from both No. 14 and No. 15 Fore Street. Charles Lewis took over the grocery and wine merchant business at No. 15, running it as the West Somerset Stores. Lewis died in 1906.

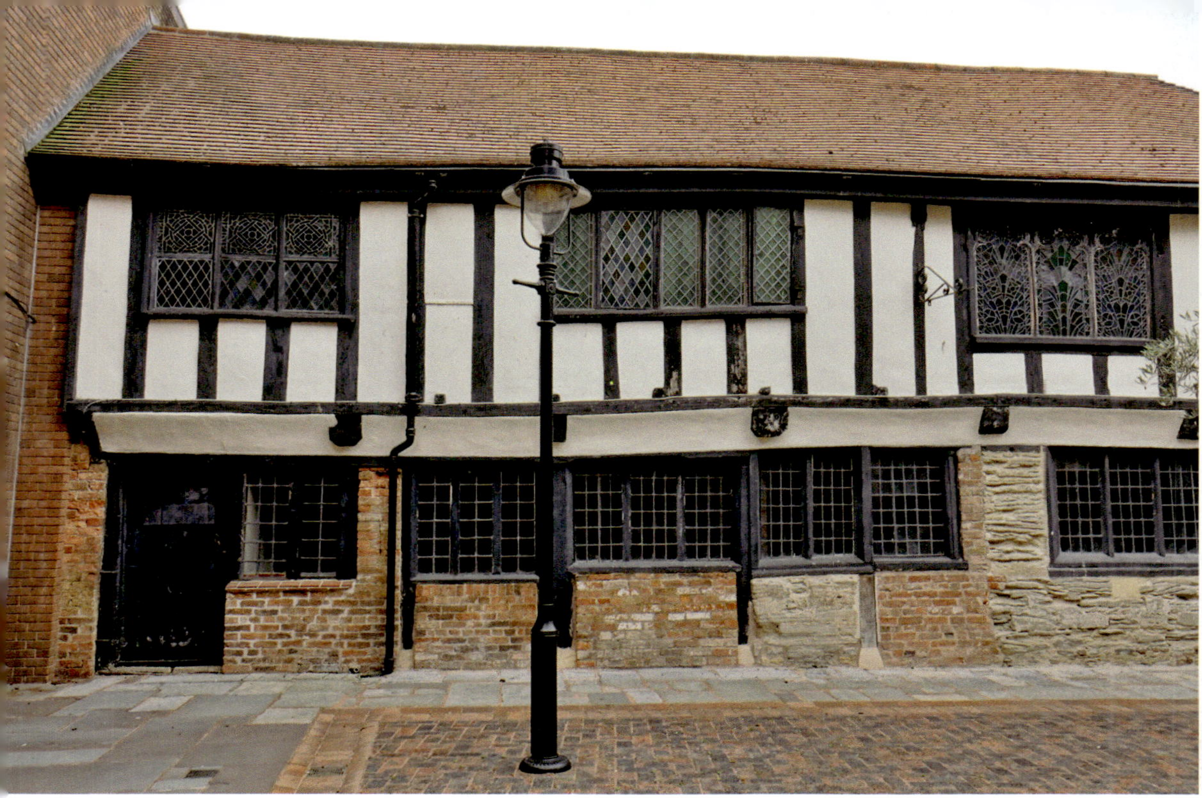

Above: This building to the rear dates to 1350 and was known as Hangman's Bar during part of the twentieth century.

Below: Lewis and Lewis at Nos 13/14, with the West Somerset Stores at No. 15 Fore Street. (Courtesy of Mates)

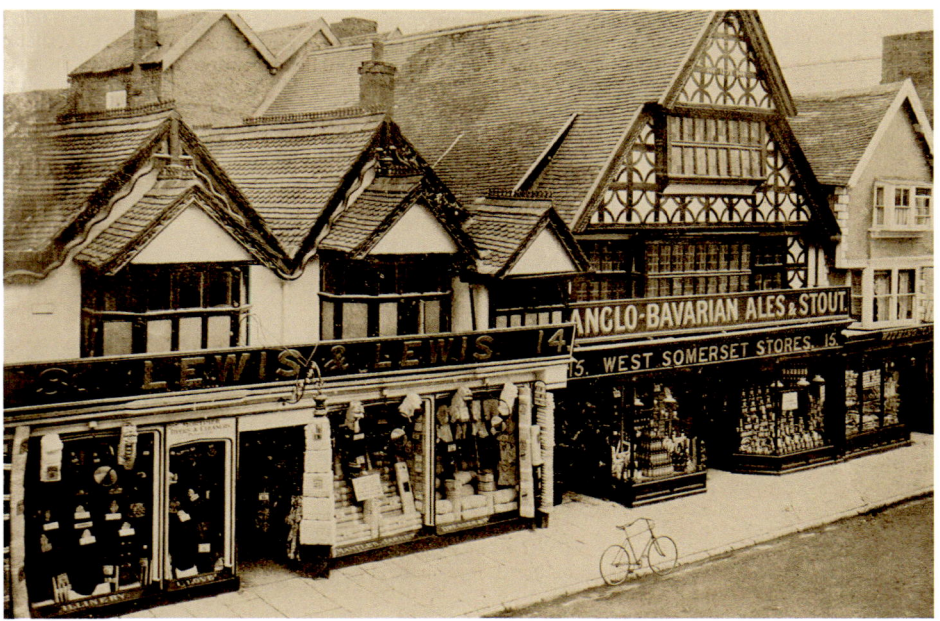

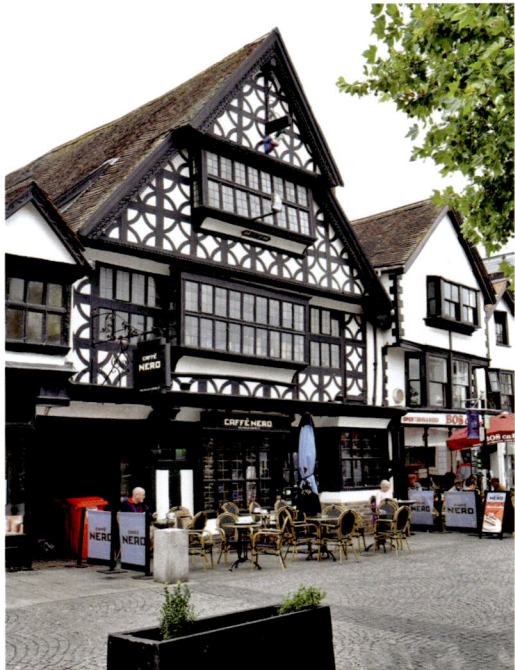

No. 15 is now a popular Caffè Nero.

Following Lewis, Halliday's Antique Shop offered services to furnish holiday cottages in the area. Halliday sold to Frank Warr & Co., Birmingham, in 1946 for use as a restaurant. R. F. Boggett bought the premises in the 1950s and, unable to make alterations, sold to Berni Inns, who opened the first steakhouse in the town. At its peak there were eight bars and three restaurants run by Berni Inns in this and the neighbouring building.

8. Municipal Buildings, 1522

The Municipal Buildings are situated on Corporation Street and although the current building was constructed in 1894, the earliest part of the building is thought to date from around 1480.

There is documentary evidence there was a school here from as early as 1286, which Bishop Richard Fox may have been responsible for rebuilding and reinvigorating during the sixteenth century. He provided an endowment to fund the schoolmaster and the initials 'R. F.' with date '1522' are carved in stone over the doorway. At one time the arms of Hugh Oldham, Bishop of Exeter, were also displayed.

The eastern end of the building is the oldest, with rubble walls and an open timber roof; this was the schoolroom. Now open to the rafters, the original structure can be appreciated but at one time this did have a ceiling. To the western

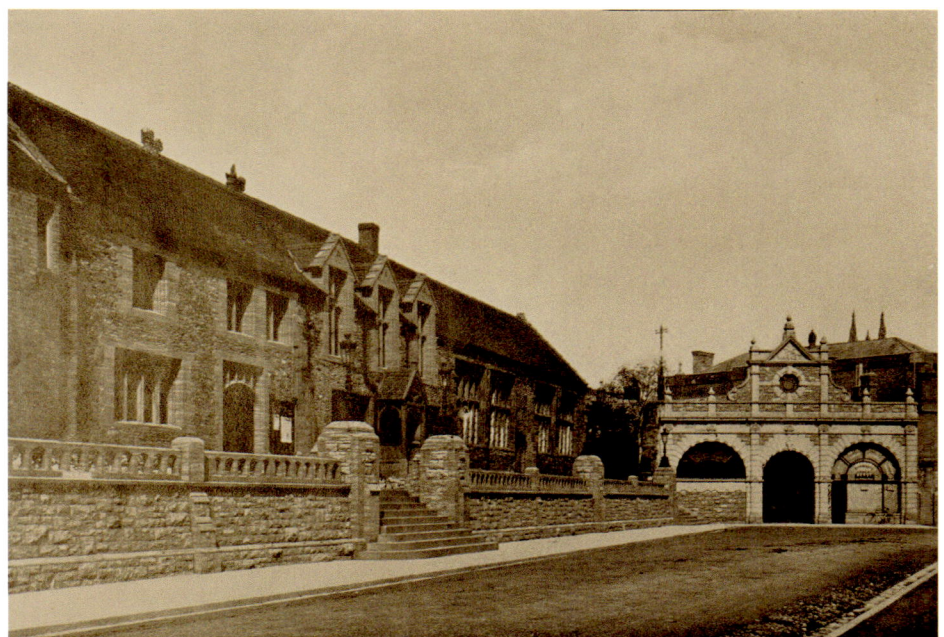

Above: The Municipal Buildings and the former entrance to the market on Castle Green, *c.* 1903. (Courtesy of Mates)

Right: The side entrance with a worn coat of arms above the doorway.

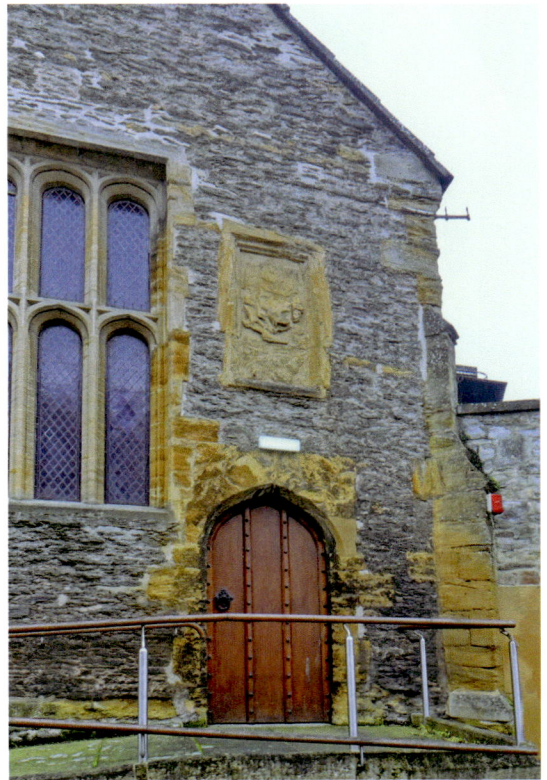

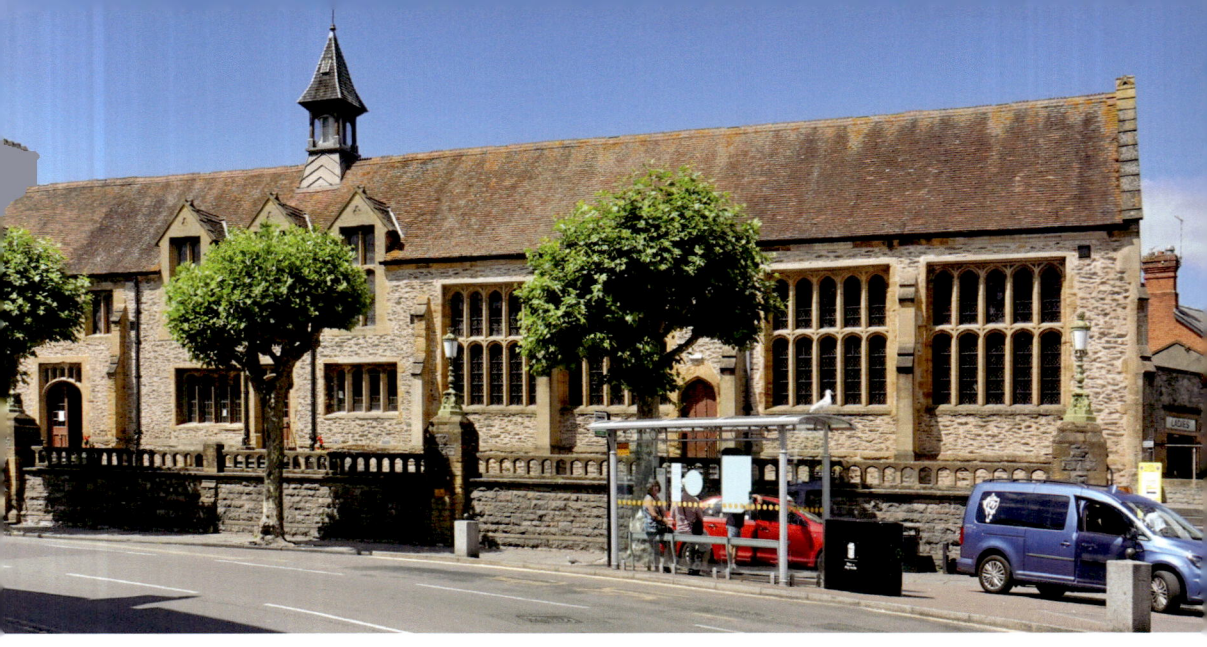

Note the feature tower added onto the roof, possibly during the 1905 Tudor-style alterations.

end, the building provided accommodation which included a master's room, perhaps also for an assistant, staff and boarders. Evidence points to this side of the building being a kitchen at one time with a medieval fireplace on the north wall.

When the school closed in 1885 the building was purchased by Taunton Town Council, who moved in during 1887 and used it as their municipal building. Alterations after this date included a Council Chamber and an impressive staircase in a wing to the north. In 1904 a Tudor-style extension was added. It may have been at this point that the ceiling in the schoolroom was removed.

When the council moved out in 1987 the building was used by voluntary bodies, and the former schoolroom for public meetings.

Since 2007 it has been the Registry Office and offers the Tudor Hall, the Vivary Room and the Somerset Room as wedding venues. The front terrace with piers and lamps is Grade II listed.

9. Waterstones (formerly The County Hotel), Sixteenth Century

The building housing Waterstones is situated on East Street and has formerly been the County Hotel, London Hotel/Inn and the Three Cups. The Three Cups is the oldest recorded inn in Taunton and was strategically placed on the former main route between London and Exeter, situated in the commercial heart of Taunton.

In 1528, John Benot, the landlord of 'le Thre Cuppys' had a licence to bake bread and his rent funded a priest at St Nicholas' Chantry within St Mary's Church – a chantry was a chapel endowed for singing Masses for the soul of the donor. During the Reformation the property was sold to London investors

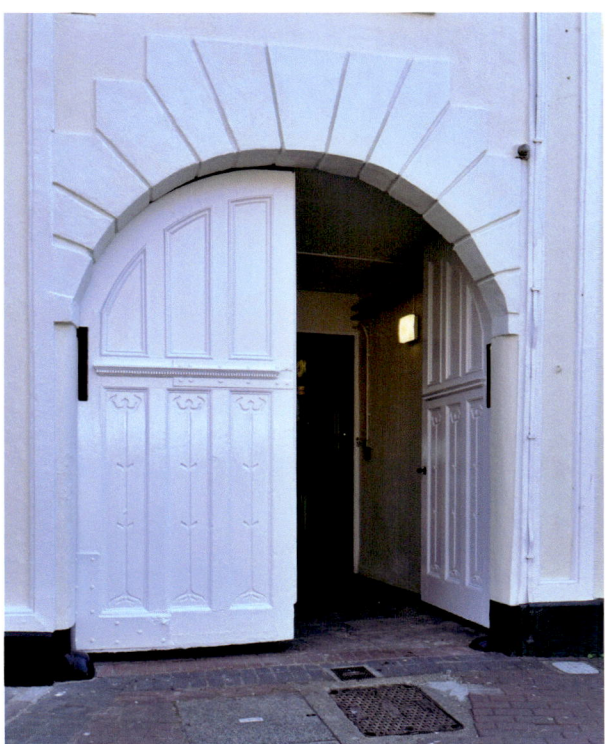

An arched carriage entryway leading to the rear of the premises, which boasted stabling for 200 horses.

and occupied by assorted landlords. Part-destroyed during the Civil War, it was repaired and partially rebuilt. Facilities included a garden and bowling green, until the owner sold part of the land for a Presbyterian meeting house.

In 1756, an auction advert described it as 'a bold and spacious entrance from East Street into a quadrangle in the centre of the house, well paved'. Coach access was from Paul Street and there was room for twenty carriages and 100 horses. The bowling green had long since become pasture for horses. The new owner, Robert Harris, held 'Butt and Cudgel' and 'Single Stick' matches, with a prize for the man who broke most heads. Harris's success was remarkable; he restored the bowling green, let post chaise (fast carriages for travelling that were drawn by two or four horses) and horses, improved facilities for 200 guests and stabling for 200 horses, with a courtyard big enough to turn a coach. A large room within the inn could be divided to hold dramatic performances.

The current building was opened in March 1784 and was later renamed the London Inn. In 1829, this was changed to 'Hotel'. An assembly room was built which in 1849 was lit by gas. Thomas George Meetens, owner and occupier, redesigned and enlarged this. An extension in 1901 added a permanent stage, dressing rooms and extra seating. A garage with an inspection pit was installed before 1905. The Tuscan porch is a feature of this building and dates to the nineteenth century.

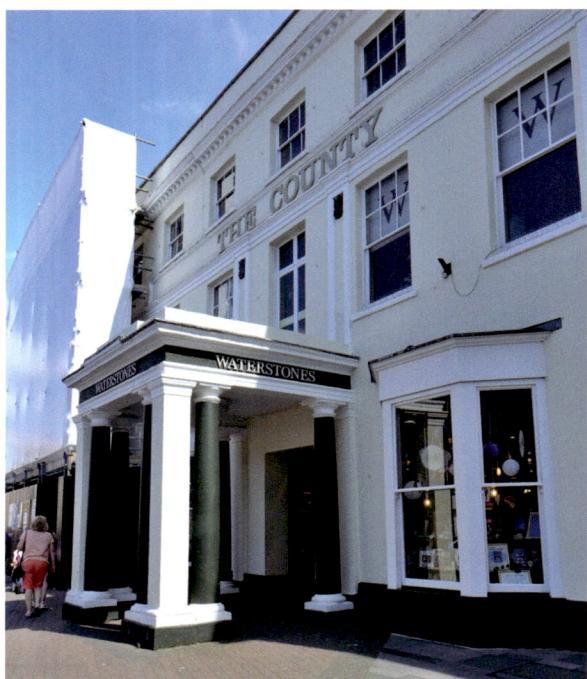

Left: The Tuscan porch entrance to Waterstones. 'The County' sign is still displayed on the front.

Below: A mid-twentieth-century postcard showing the County Hotel. To the right of the archway is now Waterstones and the left is Marks & Spencer.

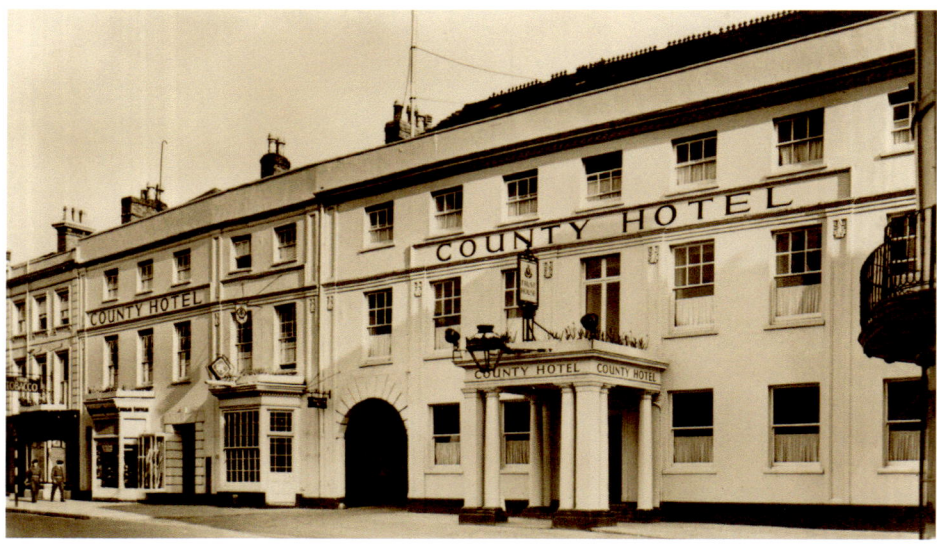

In 1919, the hotel was sold to Trust House Forte, who changed the name to the County Hotel. A cinema within the building that was trading as The Empire became the County Cinema. Upon its closure in October 1934 the rooms then became Empire Hall. In the 1990s the hotel closed and the building is now occupied by Waterstones.

10. Gray's Almshouses, 1635

Situated on East Street, these almshouses are just one of many former almshouses in the town. Built in red brick (English bond pattern) with stone mullioned windows and exceptionally tall chimneys with stacks set at an angle, they make a striking feature on the street.

They are named for their founder, Robert Gray, who was born in the town but settled in London where he became a successful businessman. In his will dated

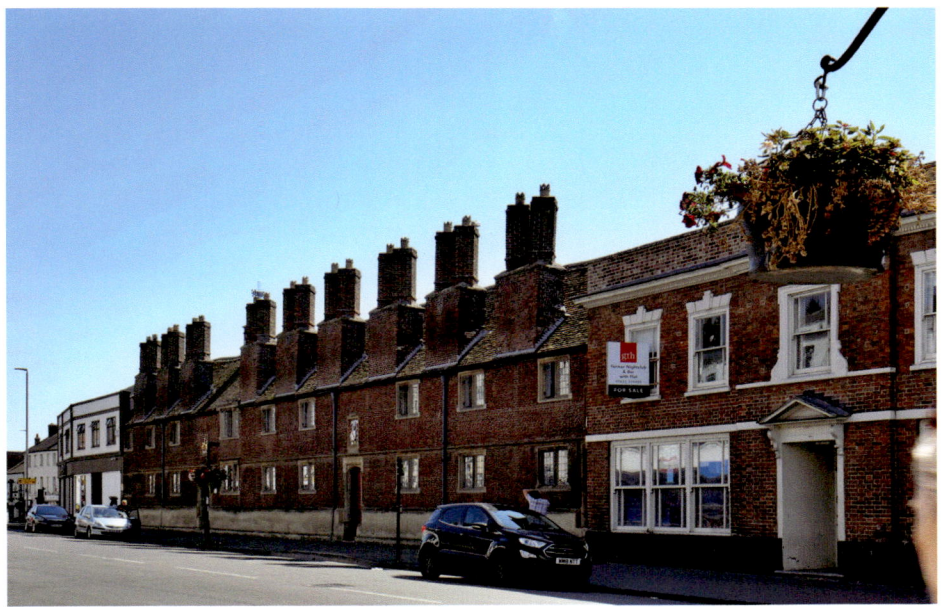

Above: Gray's Almshouses on East Street.

Right: The datestone shows the year it was founded and Robert Gray's coat of arms.

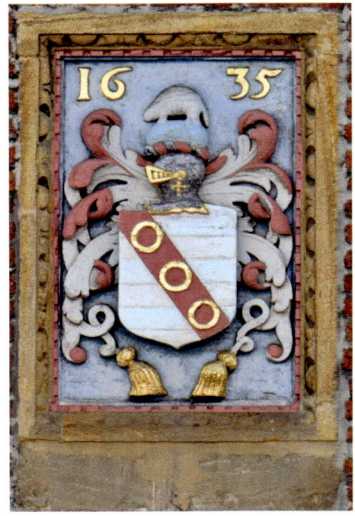

1638 one bequest was to the ten (single) almswomen and six poor almsmen in the almshouses 'in Taunton … where I was borne by me lately built'. The datestone and inscription give the year 1635. As well as seventeen apartments with gardens, there was a chapel and schoolroom where a chaplain was to teach ten poor children and pray daily in the chapel for the residents of the almshouses. In 1892, when the Huish School for Boys was built on Mount Lane part of the gardens from the almshouses was sold to give space for the school.

All the surviving almshouses in town are now run by Taunton Heritage Trust and offer accommodation for sixty-six residents in both old and new property.

11. Flook House, Seventeenth Century

Flook House is situated on Belvedere Road, Northtown, and at one time was set in its own extensive garden grounds. The original manor house dated to the seventeenth century and had a porch, mullioned windows and one overmantle that was dated 1652. In *Secret Hiding Places* (1933) Granville Squiers suggested that the house had at least two priest holes but stated that nothing could be proved. The majority of the remaining building is of eighteenth- and nineteenth-century construction.

Notable residents include John Trenchard, one-time MP for the borough and political author. Between the years 1819 and 1868 resident Dr William Metford

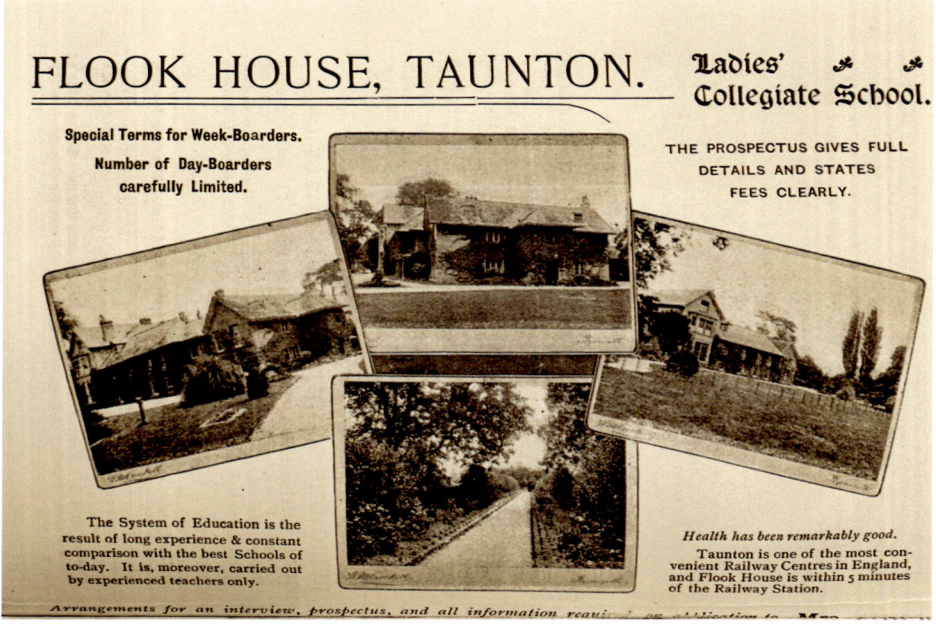

An advert for Flook House, Ladies Collegiate School, 1900. (Courtesy of Goodman)

LADIES' COLLEGIATE SCHOOL,

FLOOK HOUSE, TAUNTON.

THE SYSTEM OF EDUCATION is arranged by THOS. SIBLY, B.A., for 39 years Head Master of the Wesleyan College, and is carried out under his direction and that of Mrs. SIBLY, by their Daughters, and by experienced Resident Governesses, and non-resident Professors.

The Literary Training is as thorough and comprehensive as that offered in the higher class school for Boys.

Religious Culture, Physical Education, and the Formation of Character receive the most careful attention.

ALL APPLICATIONS TO BE MADE TO

MRS. SIBLY,

FLOOK + HOUSE, + TAUNTON.

An advert for the school from an 1883 trade directory. (Courtesy of Goodman)

was noted for his house parties that offered guests archery and rifle shooting within the grounds, which comprised a shrubbery, garden, lawn, orchard, plantations and meadow.

In 1878, Mr and Mrs Sibley moved a girls' school from its location on Kingston Road to Flook House. An advert in 1883 outlined the benefits to be gained by the daughter of prospective parents. The school closed in 1913 having offered education to the girls of the town for over fifty years.

The grounds have been used for many public events over the years, including fêtes and evening classes. By 1928 it was suggested that they should be opened to the public in perpetuity. The house and over 6 acres of park laid out by Mr Sibley were bought by Taunton Town Council for the town from Miss A. B. Sibley for £13,750, who could remain in the house as tenant for life.

The house has had many uses: County Nursing HQ/St John's Ambulance Brigade; Red Cross Hostel buildings (erected in the grounds during the war); District Registration Office of Births, Marriages and Deaths; and many volunteer-sector organisations. As the building was underused and largely redundant at the

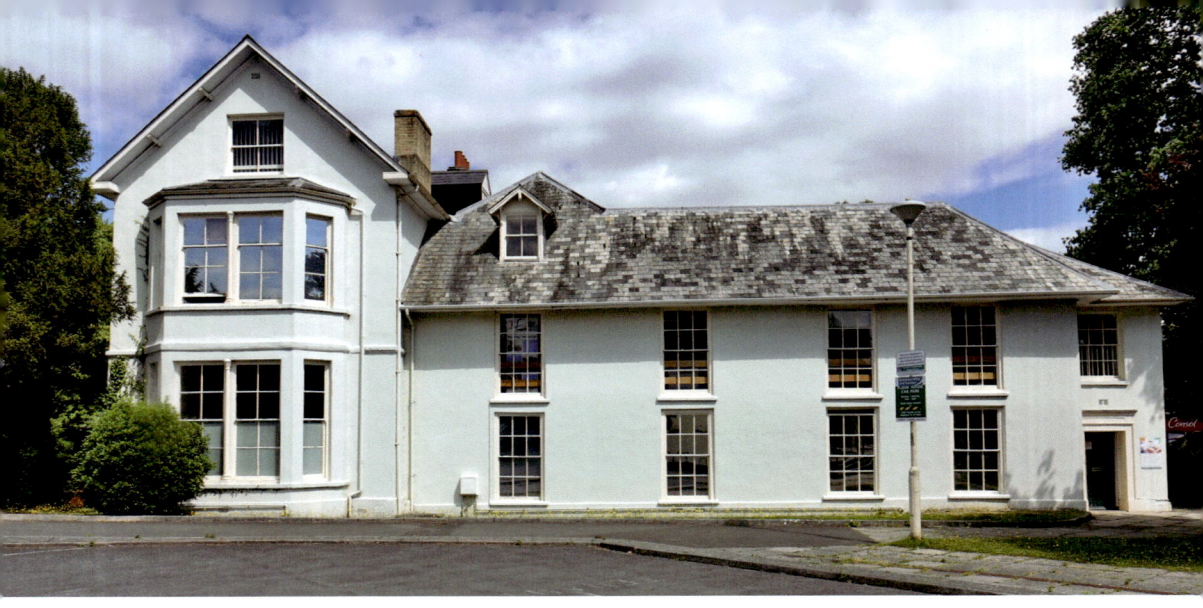

Flook House, pictured in 2022 while awaiting a decision on its future.

beginning of 2022, the council issued a grant to the Creative Innovation Centre Community Interest Company to create an art hub. This is now home to Arts Hub Taunton, where creative workshops for the community take place.

12. Unitarian Chapel, 1721

The Unitarian Chapel, Mary Street, was built in 1721 on the site of an old meeting house that may have belonged to the Baptist denomination as far back as 1646.

The interior remains largely unchanged from the eighteenth century, having full-height square Corinthian columns built with Flemish oak, oak galleries, pews and a carved pulpit. Lighting was by means of a chandelier, which was donated by the then MP for Taunton, Nathaniel Webb, in 1728.

The congregation has had some notable preachers in its time: Samuel Taylor Coleridge (who walked every Sunday from Nether Stowey in 'blue coat and brass buttons' to preach), Wesley, Dr Malachi Blake (founder of the Taunton and Somerset Hospital), and at one time the minister was Joshua Toumlin, author of *The History of Taunton*.

Unitarians have a strong belief in education for all, and in 1847 there were plans to build a schoolroom and thoroughly repair the chapel. Architects Messrs Fuller and Gingell of Bath drew up a suitable scheme for a schoolroom adjoining the chapel. When the new memorial school was built in 1886 the schoolroom was demolished to make way. This was paid for solely by the then minister, Revd J. Collins Odgers, in memory of his late wife and father-in-law, Revd William Jones. At the opening ceremony in October 1886 Revd Odgers gifted the deeds over to trustees. The Mary Street Memorial School building still stands but is now used for the homeless charity 'Open Doors'.

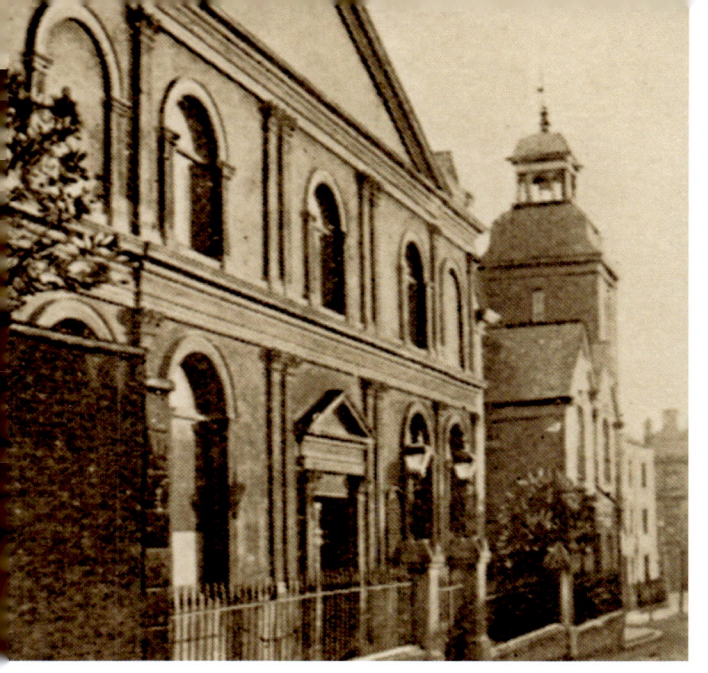 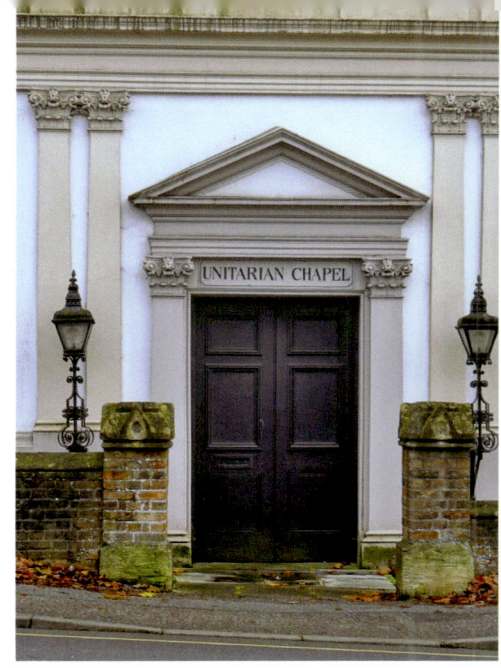

Above left: The chapel, photographed in 1903, showing the school tower. (Courtesy of Mates)

Above right: The Italianate door that was added in the 1880s.

Below: Unitarian Chapel, Mary Street.

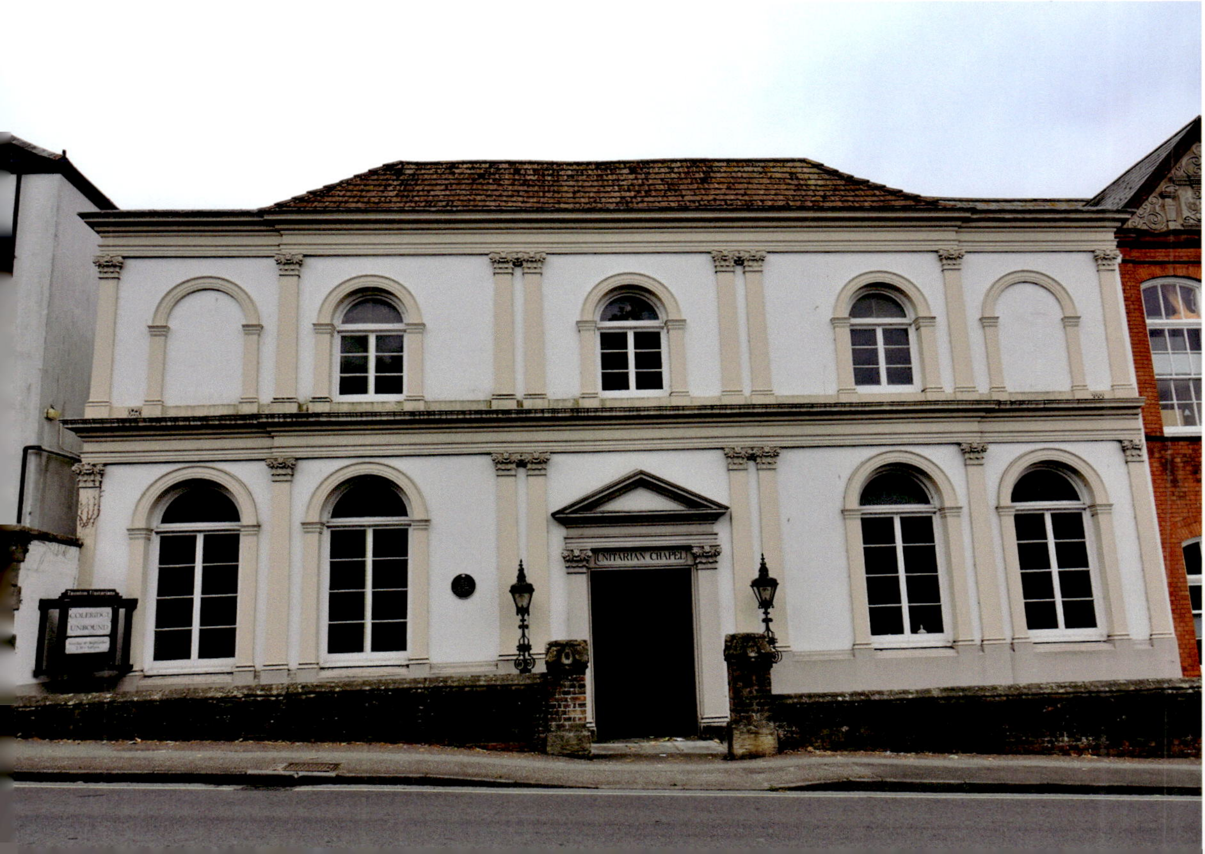

Major work in 1881 added the Italianate front, which was designed by J. Houghton Spencer. A central doorway replaced the two former entrances, and a lobby was created under the gallery.

Renovations took place in 1912 and Andrew Carnegie (famed for donations to create public libraries) donated half the money needed for a new organ.

When the 200th anniversary was celebrated in September 1921 the *Taunton Courier and Western Advertiser* reported that the celebration for the bicentenary of the building on Mary Street included meetings, services and a bazaar over two days.

13. Wilton Gaol (later Taunton Gaol), 1754

The former Wilton Gaol (later Taunton Gaol to avoid confusion with Wiltshire's Wilton Gaol) is situated along Shuttern and was built in 1754 for those committing felonies, misdemeanors or breaches of the peace. It was to house eighty prisoners and replaced the old Bridewell, or 'The Nook', which was by Tone Bridge and destroyed in 1753.

Throughout its working life the building has been altered and grown as needs have changed. Regulations that required a prisoner to have an individual cell saw architect Richard Carver brought in to execute the necessary alterations. He had also been responsible for work a decade earlier that was carried out by Herniman and Son of Eastreach; they used prisoners for much of the work, saving the county over £1,000 in labouring costs.

In February 1843, nearly 250 prisoners were transferred from Ilchester. A contemporary report stated that there was room for 350 and it was 'one of the most extensive gaols in the kingdom'. There was a chapel, infirmary, schoolroom, refractory cells, and workshops with a governor's house. Along Burton Place a new stable, millhouse and treadwheel building were constructed of single-storey height.

The remaining octagonal tower, visible from Burton Place, housed a central hall with a water tower above and a hospital. When the courts were built across the road an underground passageway was constructed, which is now used for utility services. The Prisons Act of 1877 resulted in closure in 1884 and the civil prison was moved to Shepton Mallet. For some time the premises were leased to the War Department and continued to serve as a military prison. Redundant for twenty years, the building was brought back into use in 1909 when the council decided that the police, local taxation staff and weights and measures could be accommodated in the building, and that land at the back could be let to the County Territorial Association.

In 1943, the police station was extended, then in the 1970s buildings were demolished to create parking space. By 2018 the police station was finally closed and moved to Deane House, Belvedere Road.

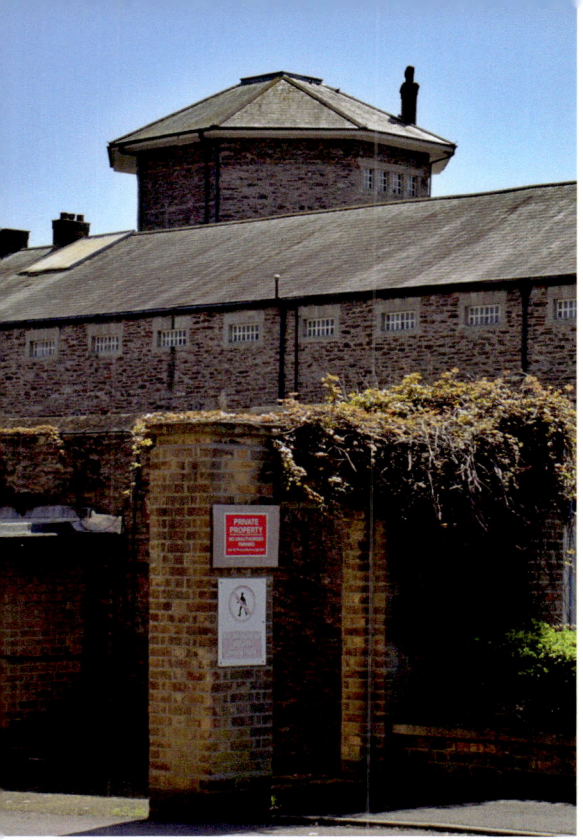 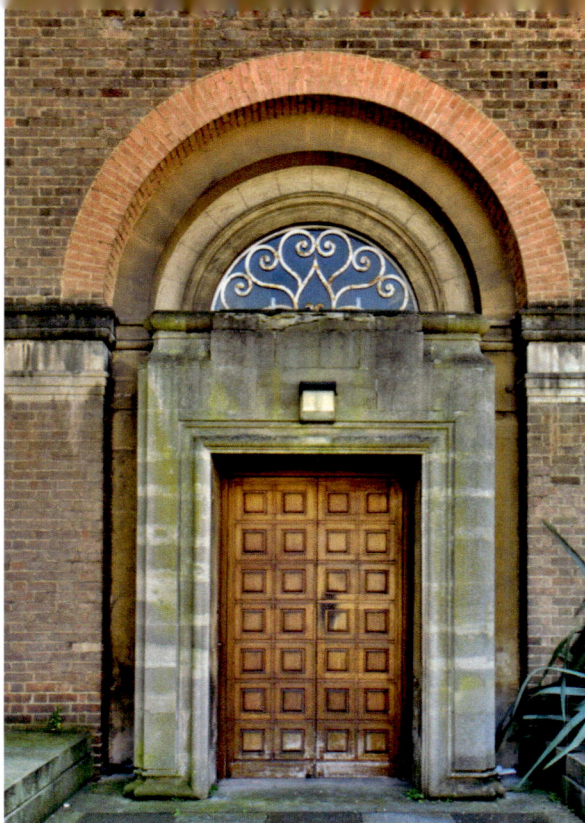

Above left: The original octagonal tower and remaining buildings of the former Wilton Gaol.

Above right: The grand entrance to the former police station.

14. Market House, 1770s

The Market House is situated in the heart of the town, where several roads converge. Despite the development of transport systems, the market has stood central for centuries.

Taunton's market was first recorded in the Domesday Book (1086) and by the mid-thirteenth century it was centred in this area. By 1682 an assembly room on pillars had been erected and a large number of public houses, the Guildhall, market cross and 100 fixed market standings were within a short distance. The Market Trustees, formed around 1768, bought the area and redeveloped old, dilapidated buildings with a design by Coplestone Warre Bampfylde of Hestercombe Court. This building of red brick, stone dressing and slate roof was completed in 1772. In Savage the market house was recognised as one of the few buildings that offered facilities for entertainment with its Guildhall, reading, billiards, card and assembly rooms.

A broad flagstone path measuring 216 feet ran between two market areas and formed The Parade. Two arcades were built to accommodate farmers and trade, whilst to the front were moveable stands for the 'flesh' market and butchers.

Markets were held on Saturdays and Wednesdays, and glovers, hatters, ropers, bakers, confectioners would sell their wares alongside the meat traders. In 1822, the butchers moved into the New Market House. Later, fruit, vegetables and books were added to the variety of goods on offer.

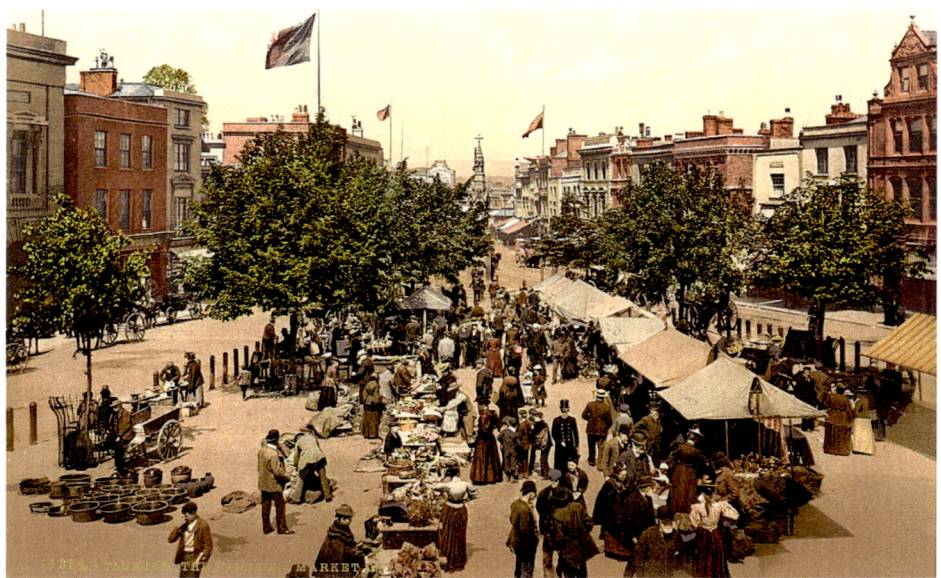

The Parade *c.* 1895, showing the market stalls either side of the broad path leading from the Market Hall. (Courtesy of Detroit)

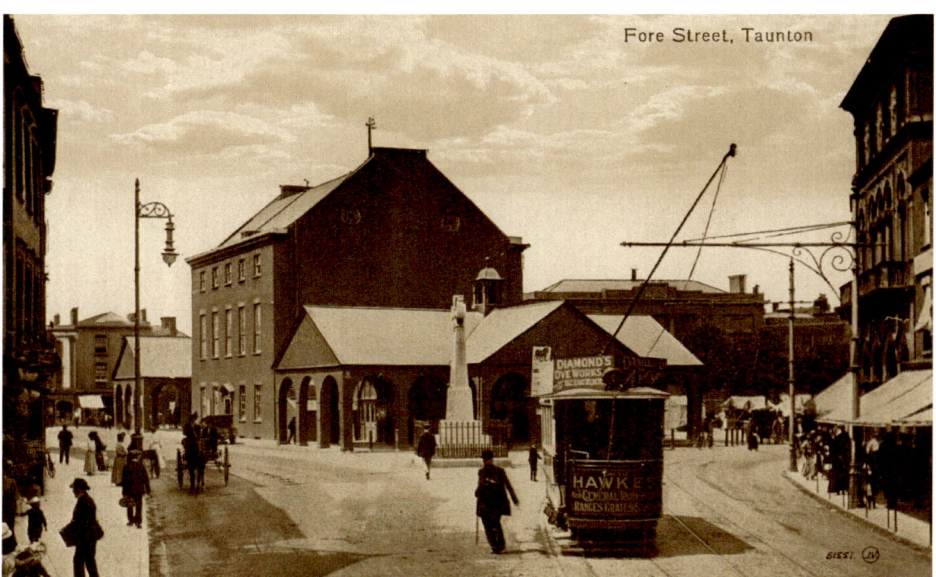

A pre-1930 postcard showing the former arcades to the side.

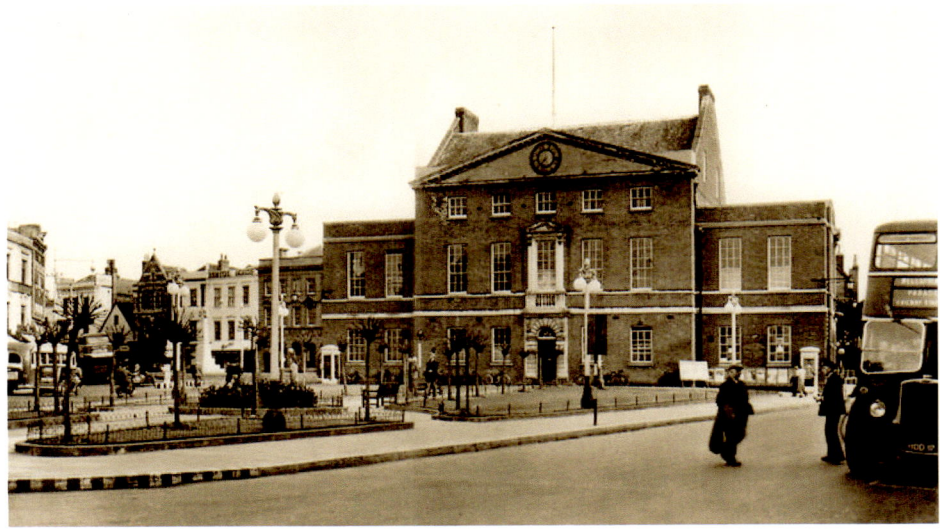

Alterations to both the Market House and road layout can be seen in this 1946 postcard.

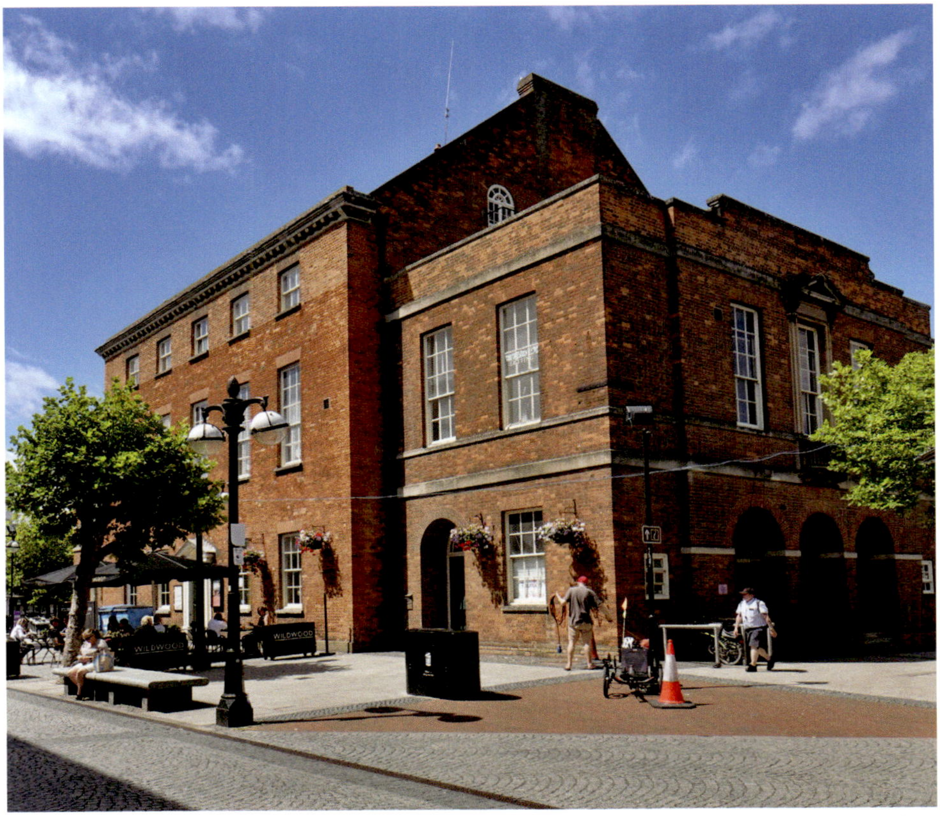

Market House viewed from Fore Street showing the altered arcades.

The trustees handed the market over to Taunton Corporation in 1926 and trading continued until 1929 when the market was moved to Jarvis Field on Priory Bridge Road.

The years 1885/86 saw the addition of six cast-iron lamp standards – three on each side of The Parade. These lamps were the first electric street lighting in the south-west and were demonstrated by Henry Massingham using equipment provided by American company Thomson-Houston. The cost to Massingham, who paid for the whole installation, was £5,000. In 1996, the lamps were moved to their current position on the south side of the Market House.

In 1930, the arcades were demolished so that the road could be expanded, and in 1932 more significant changes were made with the addition of the new two-storey wings.

15. Franciscan Convent, 1772

The convent on South Road was originally built as a hospital, but it was never finished due to lack of funds. The foundation stone was laid by the then prime minister, Frederick North, on 29 September 1772, followed by a ball in the evening. Mr James Coles then bought the property for use as a private residence and completed the building, but it proved inconvenient as a home. He called it The Lodge, a name that was used by the next owners.

These owners were to be an order of Franciscan nuns residing in Winchester. They were refugees from the French Revolution who settled in Winchester in 1794 after leaving Bruges, Belgium. In order to make the building suitable for their use many

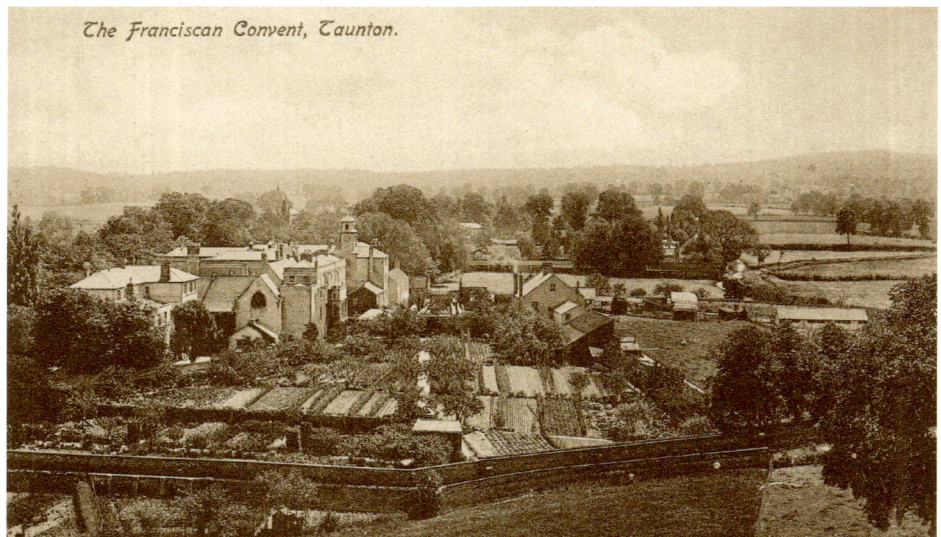

A general view of the convent showing extensive productive gardens.

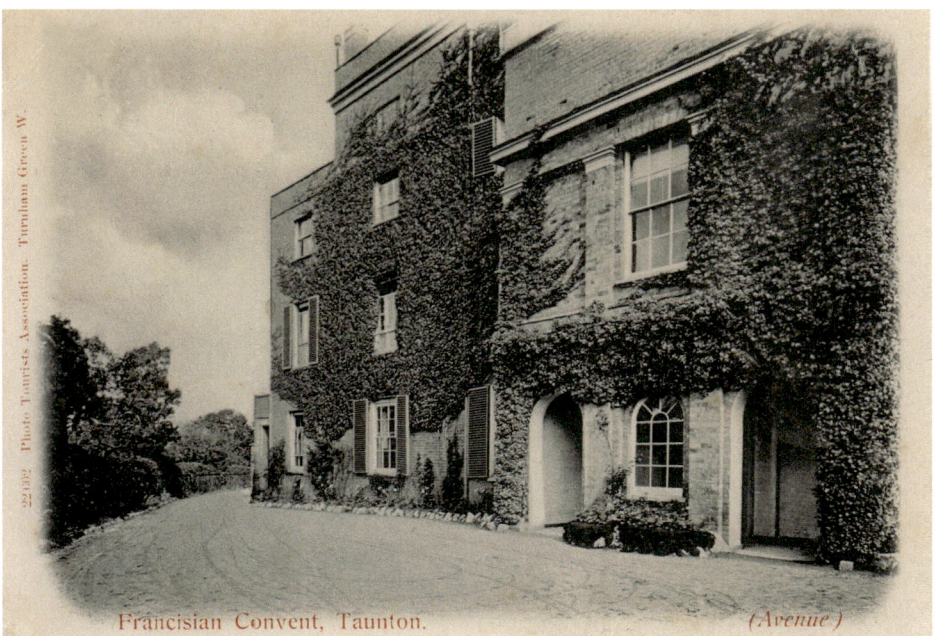
The front of the convent.

alterations were needed. Over the following years much was spent on repairs and conversions. The original symmetrical building was built in red brick and a later central addition was in yellow brick. This extension has a bowed end. A bell tower and a Gothic-style chapel and cloister were all added over time. Neighbouring land was bought to be used as both vegetable and ornamental gardens.

Due to a reduction in the number of Franciscan nuns the convent was sold to the Sisters of St Joseph of Annecy. It reopened as St Joseph's Convent School, which thrived throughout the 1950s and 1960s. This closed in 1978 and became part of King's School. The building has now been converted into flats, with the block named Annecy Court.

16. Hatcher & Sons, 1775

Hatcher & Sons, now situated at Nos 9–13 High Street, is one of the oldest department stores trading in Taunton. Established in 1775 as a draper, by 1846 it was trading as Newberry & Blake. Mr Hatcher joined the company before 1860, when it was trading as Newberry, Blake & Hatcher. When Mr Blake retired in 1883, a partnership of twenty-three years was dissolved and the new name became Hatcher & Sons.

During the nineteenth century many different trades were listed in town directories and advertisements: upholsterers, carpet factors, cabinet makers, general drapers, silk mercers, funerals 'completely furnished', general house furnishers, milliners, mantle makers, indoor and outdoor blinds, glass and china merchants, hairdressers and more.

In 1887, Taunton Electric Lighting Company installed telephone communications between the drapery business on the High Street and the carpet and furniture shop at The Parade. By 1908 there were eight separate premises. Some of these were the depository on Kingston Road, No. 33 The Parade, Nos 13–15 Hammet Street and

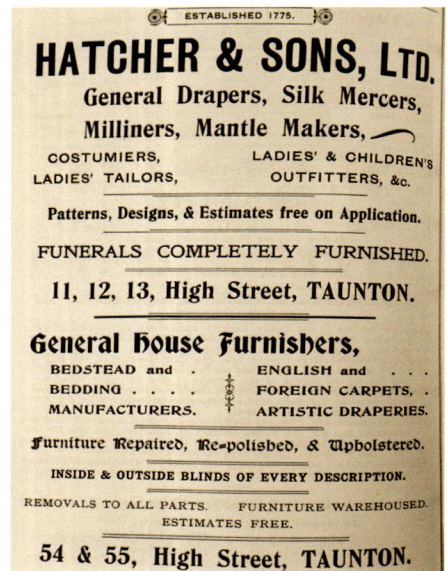

Left: A typical Hatchers advert from a 1900 trade directory. (Courtesy of Goodman)

Below: The tympanum above Nos 54–55 High Street, now Tesco Express.

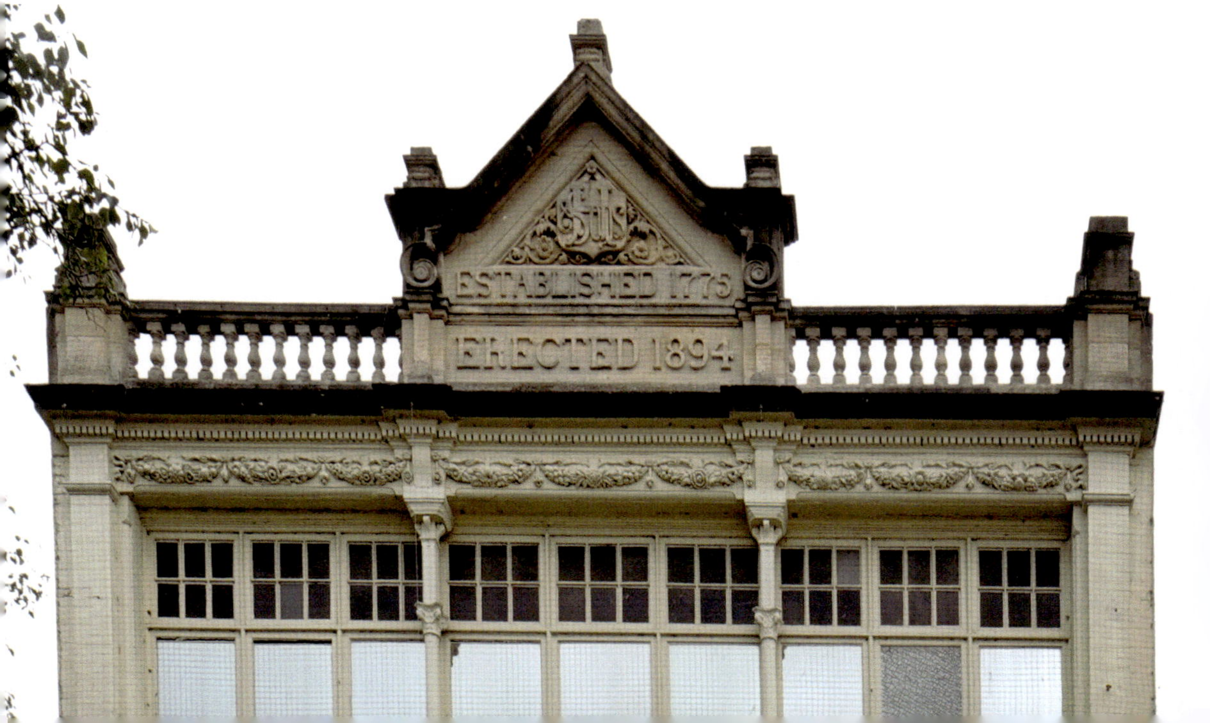

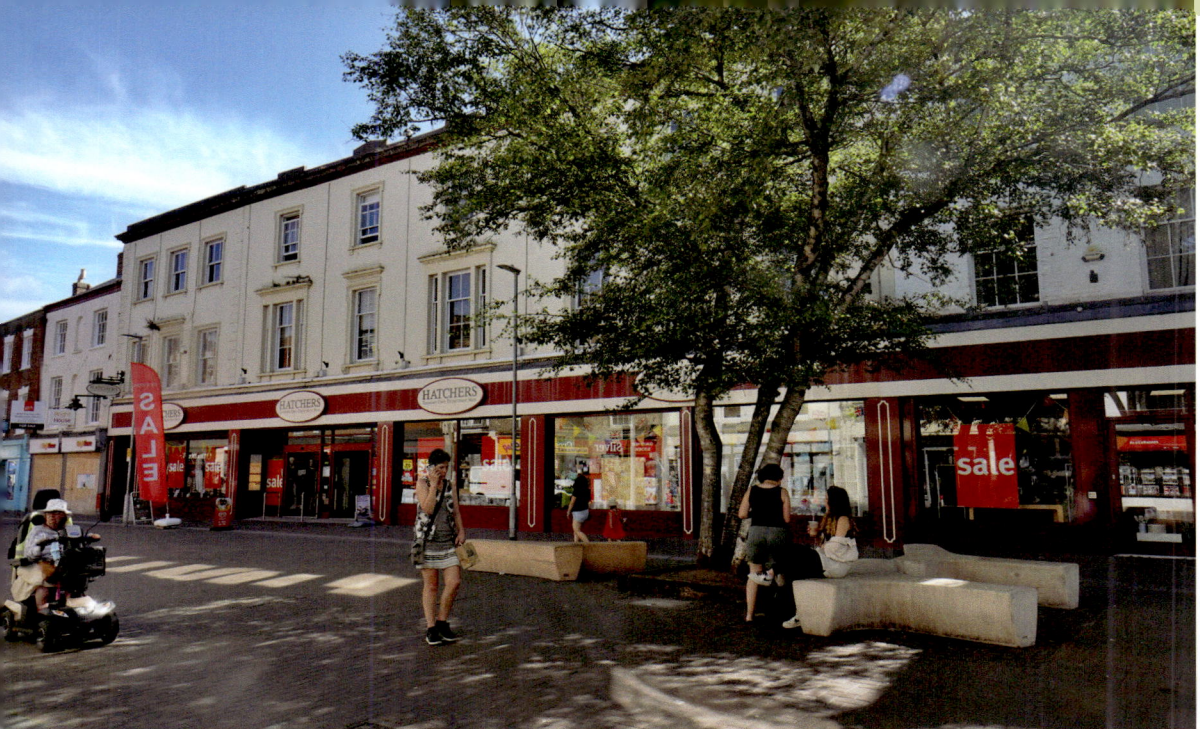

Hatchers' current store at Nos 9–13 High Street, which used to include units to the south of Pig Market Lane.

multiple units on High Street. One such premises at Nos 54–55 High Street (now a Tesco Express store) was built in 1894 according to the tympanum (a vertical recessed triangular space forming the centre of a pediment, usually decorated), which also notes the foundation year of the company.

Still run by the same family, the firm now trades from the one unified store on High Street.

17. Octagon Chapel, 1776

The Octagon was built by Mr Perrett (a London builder settled in Taunton) as a preaching house and was opened on 6 March 1776 by John Wesley, who had been visiting the town since 1743 and continued to do so until 1789. Wesley's preference was for octagonal chapels with separate male and female areas. Toumlin described the building as being 40 feet diameter with twelve windows, six of which were round. The land was conveyed by John Ridge to the Wesleyans two years later for £100 'on part of which is lately erected a Chappell or House for publick Worship for the people called Methodists, known by the name of the Octagon Chappell'.

As the congregation grew it was necessary to expand the building, and in 1796 galleries were installed. The expansion continued and by 1812 they had moved to new premises at The Temple, Upper High Street, whilst letting the Octagon to another Nonconformist congregation until 1827. The Wesleyans used it as a schoolroom but then sold it in 1831 for £360 to clear debt on The Temple. The auction advert described the freehold land on which the brick-built chapel was situated as 'adjoining St James's Place, with a frontage of 55 feet 6 inches, enclosed with Iron Fences and Walls, and nearly 100 feet in depth'.

The building was occupied by various Nonconformist groups until the Plymouth Brethren finally settled in the building, remaining there until 1965 when they moved to the newly built Octagon Chapel on East Reach. The schoolrooms suffered a fire in March 1905 that destroyed the roof and matchboarding, which was replaced with tiles; the ceilings were plastered and the roof was raised. Local builder Mr H. J. Spiller, an ecclesiastical and general builder based on Bridge Street, completed the work in three months.

Eventually the old building was sold and used for warehousing for Oxfam. At one time it was The Camelot Club, and around 1990 was developed into office space, which it was used as until it was sold in 2012. Surrounding the former chapel is a 1980s flat development.

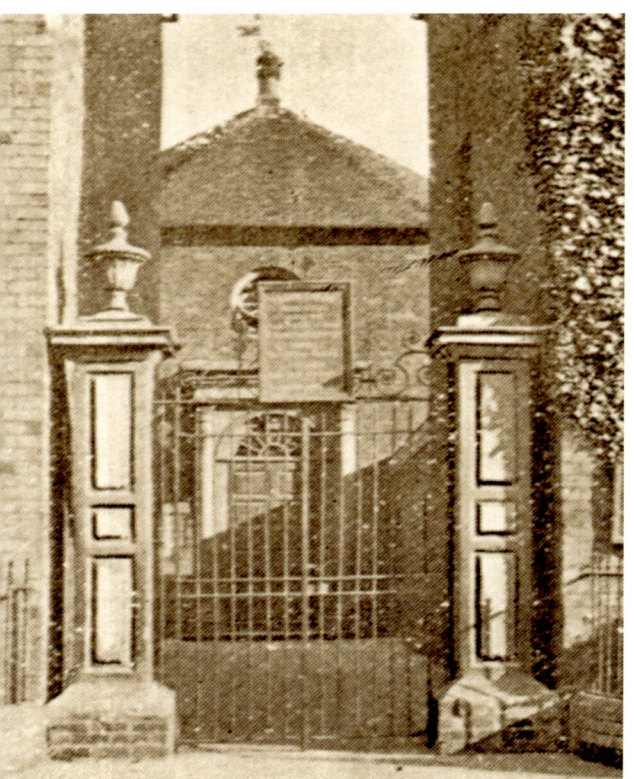 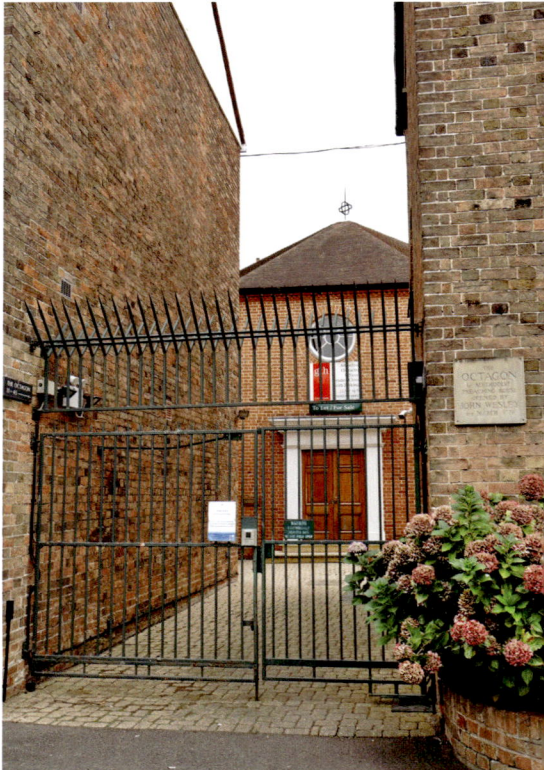

Above left: This 1903 image shows the pillars either side of the narrow access lane to The Octagon. (Courtesy of Mates)

Above right: The entrance in 2022. Have the pillars been removed or destroyed?

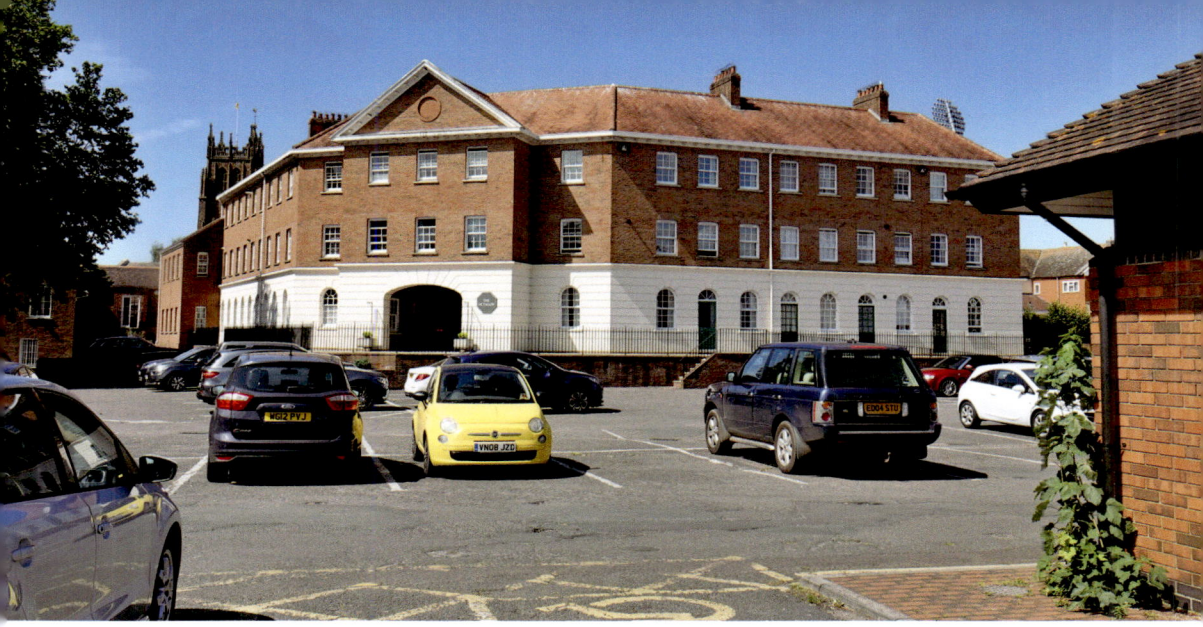

The Octagon housing development (built *c.* 1988) surrounds the chapel.

18. Hammet Street, 1788

Sir Benjamin Hammet was a London banker who became Taunton's MP shortly after building Hammet Street. In order to build the street, Hammet had to have a bill passed through Parliament – the Taunton Improvement Act 1788. This was protested against by the parishioners as it involved demolishing both Henley's and Huish's Almshouses and losing market storage and cleaning space.

The old houses were occupied by 'unsavoury persons' and were replaced with elegant houses for the use of 'genteel families out of trade'. A previously narrow alley described as a 'dirty crooked lane' was widened out to allow carriages to pass on their way up to the church. The view towards the church is probably the best-known view of Taunton.

The terraces of three-storey Georgian houses were faced with brown brick. They had sash windows and slate and tile roofs with guttering and drainpipes, which can still be seen.

In 1817, No. 12 was the home of Mrs Gatcombe. A sale of her household goods and furnishings (a normal practice at this time when one was moving house) took place on the premises. In May 1824, Mrs and Miss Barnes of Honiton moved their school into No. 12, which was to reopen after the midsummer recess on 19 July. Both boarding and day pupils were taken.

Some of the other residents and trades at No. 12 have been: Monsieur Jules A. le Franc in 1834, who offered French and fencing lessons from either 'his premises or abroad' (this term refers to the pupil's own home), and would attend schools and academies; Mr Coker, dental surgeon, in 1834; and Mrs Fatcher, dress and mantle-making establishment, in 1872.

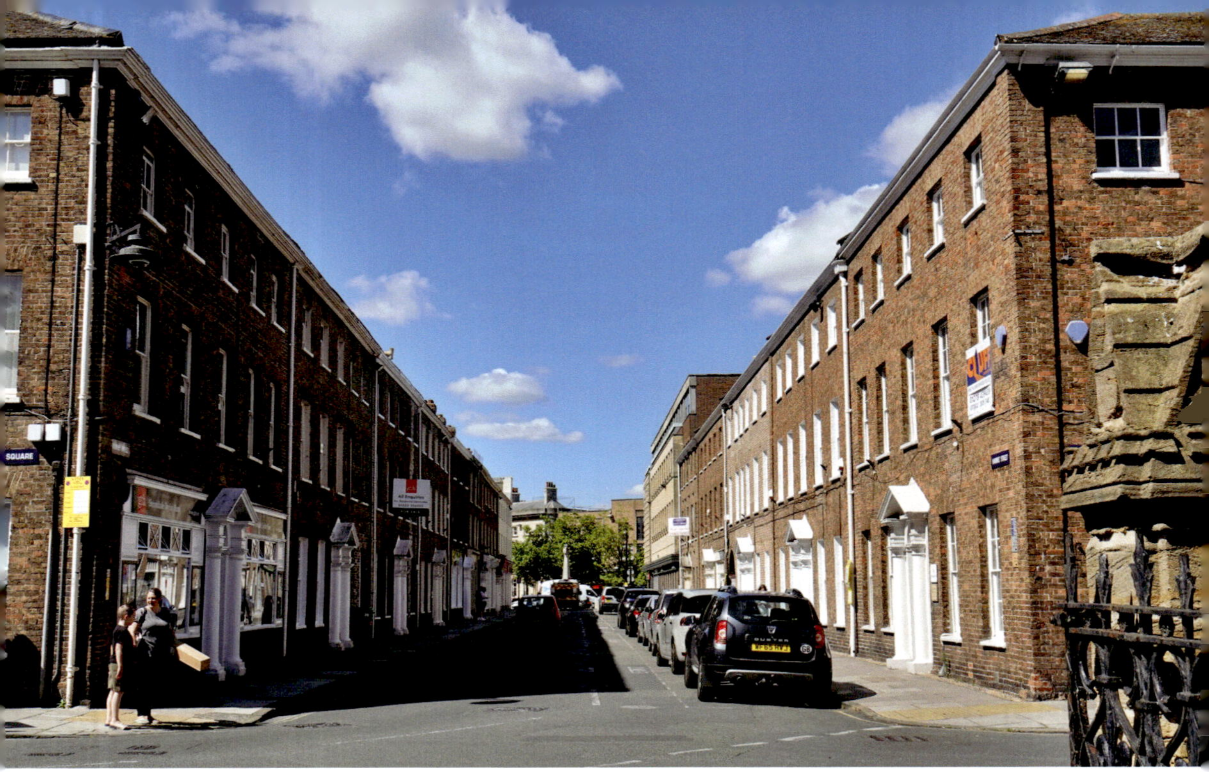

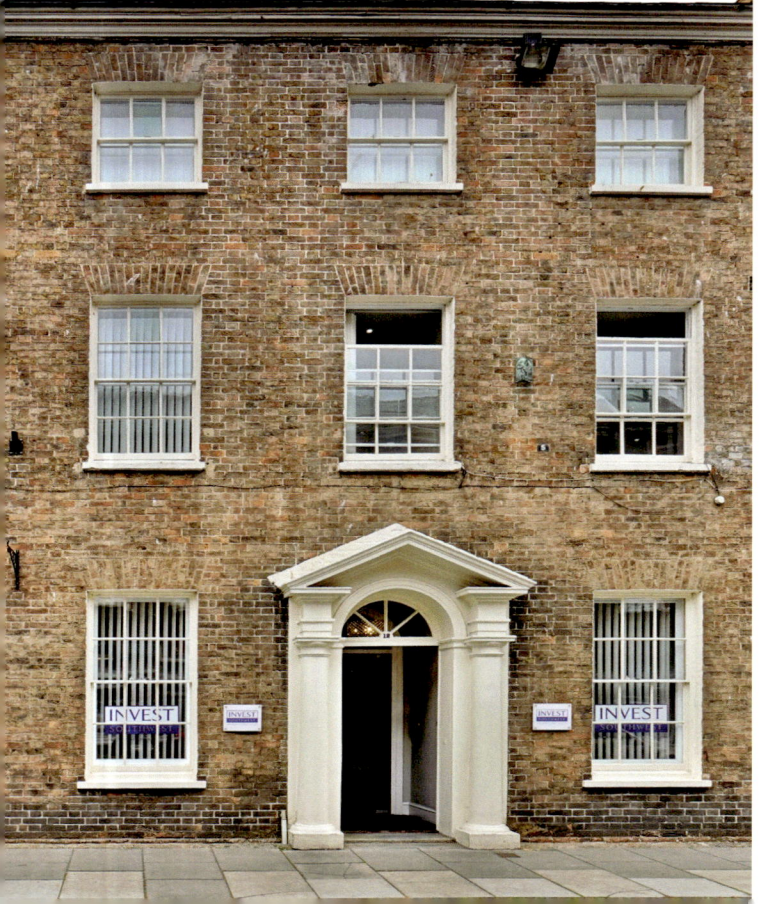

Above: Hammet Street viewed from Taunton Minster.

Left: The symmetry of each property means it blends seamlessly into the next.

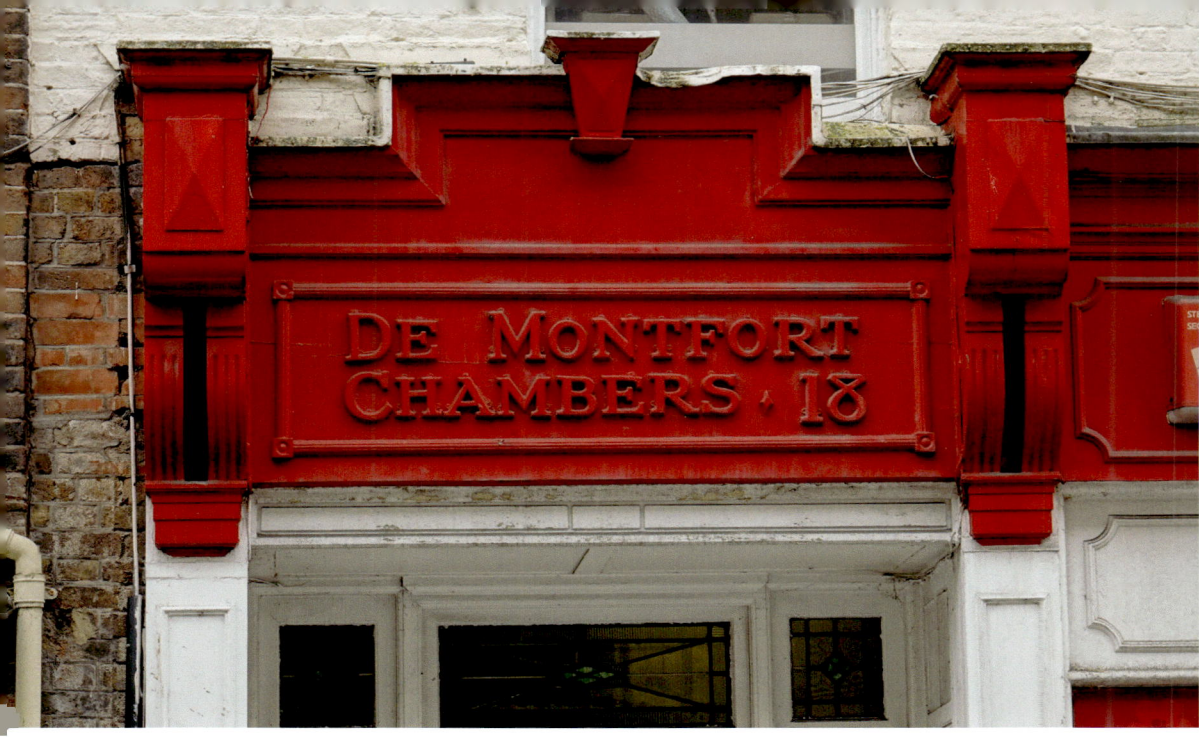

No. 18 Hammet Street. In the 1940s this was land and estate agent company Deacon and Evans.

When No. 11 was offered to be let in 1819 the property consisted of a drawing room, dining room, breakfast parlour, six bedrooms and 'all convenient offices' (this would refer to rooms such as servants' quarters, a kitchen, scullery, etc.). In the same advert No. 9 was also to be let, but it had eight bedrooms.

These days solicitors' offices and estate agents predominate.

19. United Reformed Church, 1797

The early Presbyterian church had a troubled time and ministers were open to imprisonment. George Newton and Joseph Alleine (assistant to Newton from 1655) were ejected from the parish church of St Mary for their beliefs in 1662 and founded the congregation now known as the United Reformed Church. Alleine was imprisoned several times for his continued preaching of the gospel. The first church building on Paul Street was built on land donated by Rawlin Mallack of Devon, and of the County Hotel, East Street. By the 1730s the congregation was moving towards Congregationalism, and in 1796 it joined the newly formed Somerset Association of Independent Churches which was later to become the Somerset Congregational Union.

The current church building was erected in 1797 of red brick with ashlar dressings and a slate roof at a cost of £2,000. In 1877 the two side porches replaced the three original doorways and internal improvements included the addition of gas lighting and hot air heating.

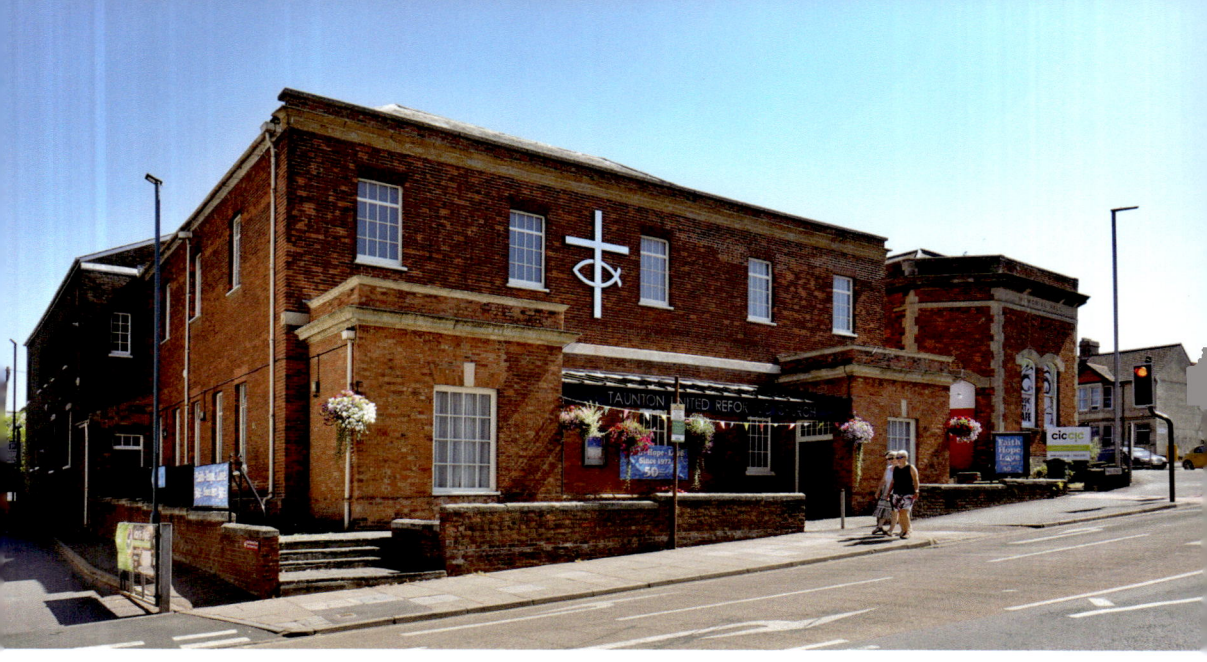

The United Reformed Church, Paul Street.

In 1862 the adjacent Memorial Hall was built marking the 200th anniversary of the founding of the congregation by Newton and Alleine. This is now the home of the Creative Innovation Centre Community Interest Company (CICCIC).

20. Bath Place

Bath Place was an ancient footway named Hunt's Court after property owner Hugh Hunt, who sold to Benjamin Hammett in 1791. In *Recollections of Old Taunton*, Goldsworthy recounts just how dirty and smelly this alleyway was:

> Very narrow, with houses on both sides and very near each other. At the bottom of it close to the archway, was an open drain, wherein all the abominations from the courts in High Street and the Crescent houses were seen passing down. This drain had nothing but a very unsafe door (generally open) to prevent people from falling into it. It was a rough and dirty court, having only a narrow strip of pavement in the middle, with flint stones on one side, and flint stones and a dirty gutter on the other.

In 1834, following some 'oppressive weather' Hunt's Court was rendered almost impassible because of uncovered gutters and disgusting drains. A newspaper reporter noted that the worthy and honourable proprietor was currently canvassing his constituents, but any visit he may make there (Bath Place) would be short due to the general condition. In 1840, the lot was sold to Mr Norman whilst there was some speculation of a new road to be built that would involve Hunt's

Court; fifty years later and this debate was still going on. Within the space of four years the name had changed to Bath Street/Place, but it was still referred to as Hunt's Court for several years. An advert for J. P. Couzens tailoring, embroidery and Parisian Hat Emporium declared their address as No. 7 Bath Place (late Hunt's Court) in 1850.

The width of the alley came to the notice of the Quarter Sessions in 1846 when the right of way for carriages came under scrutiny. The tradesmen had used carriages to bring raw materials to their premises for many years, but some were

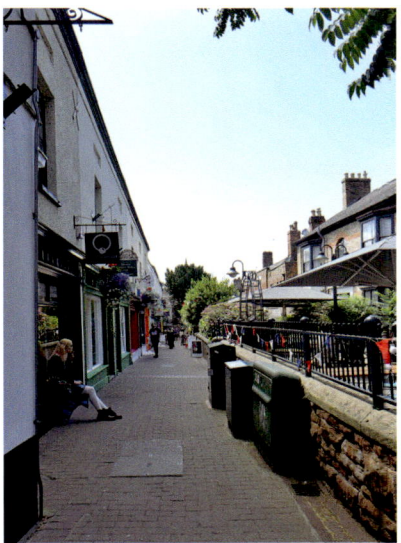

Right: A general view of Bath Place.

Below: The colourful shopfronts along one side of Bath Place.

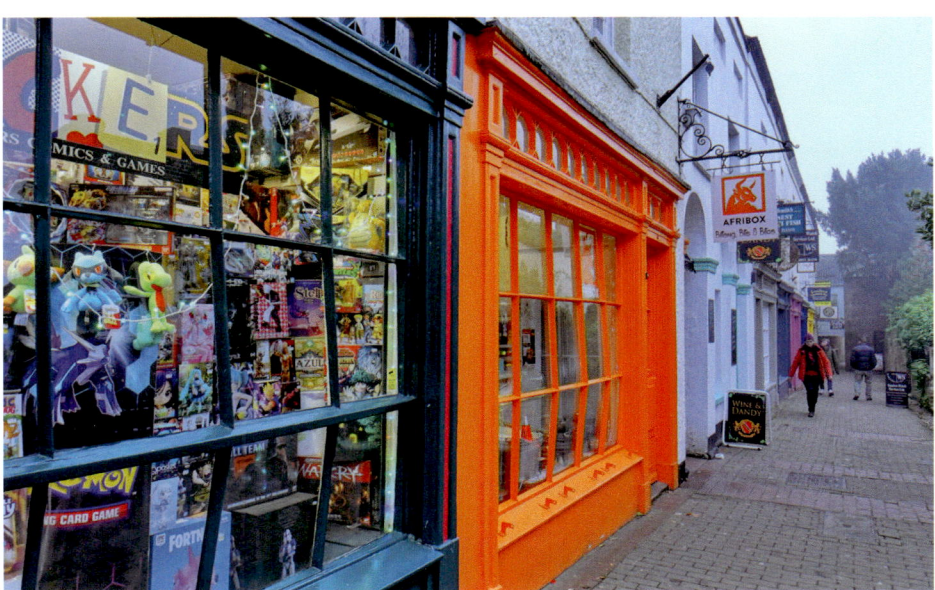

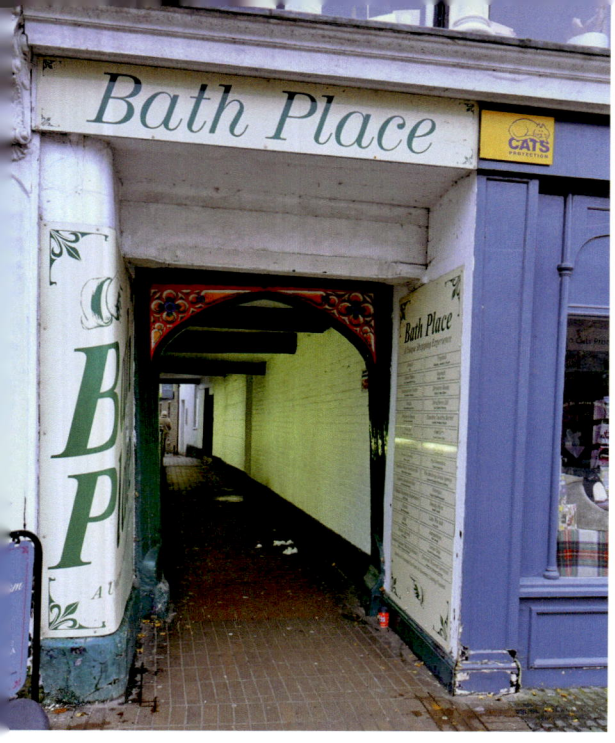

A narrow passage from High Street gives access to Bath Place.

now objecting. The judges found in favour of the tradesmen. In 1860, the road surface was found to be unsafe and the owners were called to repair it.

These days the principal attraction of this very pleasant alley is the row of twelve nineteenth-century shopfronts, which on the whole remain as they would have looked when new.

21. The Crescent, 1807

The Crescent was started in 1807 as part of town improvements that were being encouraged by Sir Benjamin Hammet prior to his death in 1800. With its barely noticeable curve, The Crescent comprises two terraces of houses that are built in a pinkish-brown-coloured brick with three storeys and a basement. Intended for genteel families, they offered a good range of comfortable rooms for both the family and the servant. In 1819, when No. 1 came up for sale it was advertised as having breakfast room, dining room, drawing room, nursery, a 'handsome stone staircase', six bedrooms and a kitchen, with all suitable and convenient offices including two water closets, coach house, a stable, walled garden, hot house with vines, and apricot and peach trees. It was supplied with good 'spring and rain water'.

The parkland in front of the street was not permitted to be built upon as it provided the residents with a pleasant outlook. Over a century later the new County Hall was built on the site, which continued to be enlarged throughout the twentieth century. The private road was gated, preventing all but residents and their visitors from access, and strategically positioned posts prevented 'corpulent persons' entering.

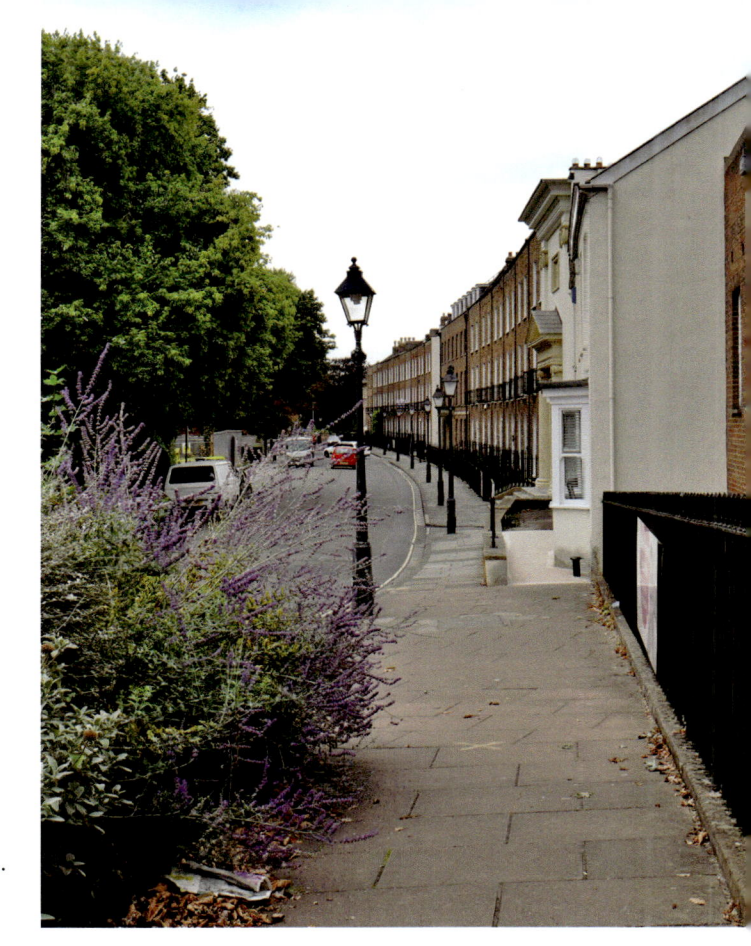

Right: The Crescent, photographed from South Road.

Below: No. 1 The Crescent.

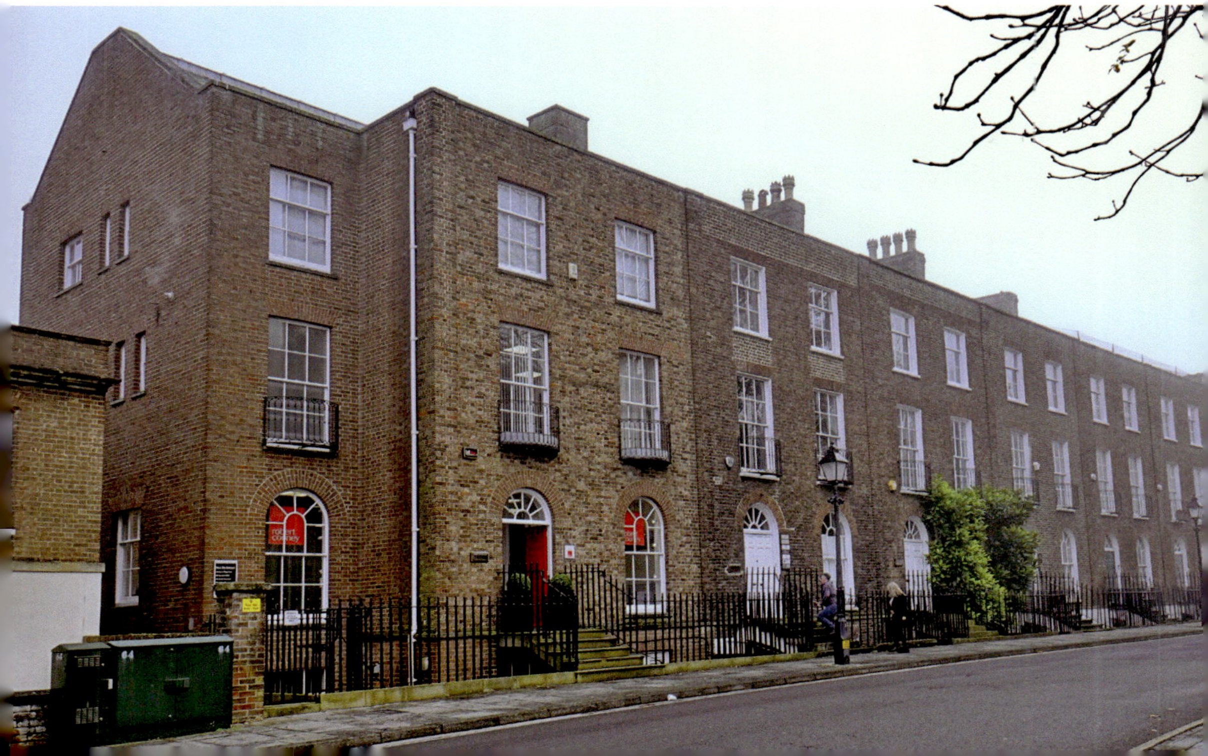

22. Taunton and Somerset Hospital, East Reach, 1810

In 1809, Dr Malachi Blake suggested establishing a county hospital for the 'relief of the sick and lame poor' to commemorate the golden jubilee of George III. Funds were raised by subscription and building commenced on land donated by Mr George Shepherd of Bishops Hull. In December 1811, two separate builders surveyed the premises and expressed their 'unqualified approbation in the manner in which Mr White the architect has fulfilled his contract'. Mr Wride, plumber and glazier of Taunton, had fitted the building with water closets and bath-showers. On 25 March 1812, the hospital opened with beds for twenty-six patients. Five nurses were on duty by day, and two by night. Subscribers could recommend four outpatients per annum for a sum of 10 guineas, or eight outpatients or one inpatient for a sum of 20 guineas.

Expansions in 1839, 1842 and 1848 were necessary and between 1870 and 1873. East and west wings were added, which expanded the capacity to ninety patients. The architect for this extension was J. Houghton Spencer of Taunton. Electric light was added in 1898 and a general modernisation in 1901 saw a passenger lift installed. In 1904, an X-ray machine was bought. Over 100 years, 43,000 patients were successfully treated.

Two doctors, Edward Liddon and William Kelly, suggested a training school for nurses to commemorate Queen Victoria's golden jubilee, and an appeal raised the necessary funds. In 1888 the Victoria Jubilee Nursing Institute opened next to the hospital offering both a home and place of study for trainee nurses.

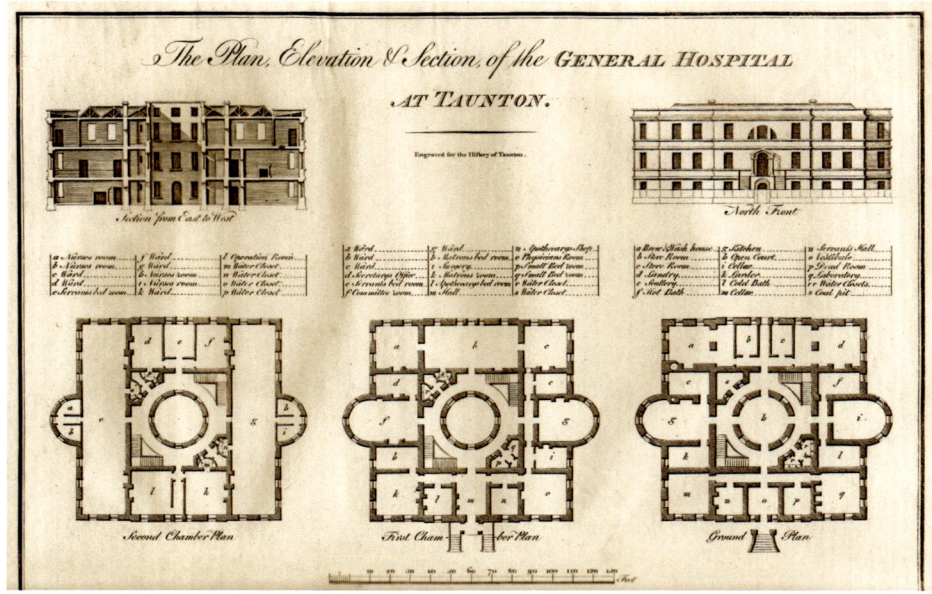

A plan of the hospital appeared in *The History of Taunton* in 1822. (Courtesy of Savage)

In 1928, the land adjacent to the nursing institute was bought from the owners of the Seven Stars Inn, which had lost its licence in 1925/26. It was planned to extend the institute's accommodation and also increase hospital space. The following year it was under debate whether they should look for alternative sites as the town grew.

In 1987, East Reach Hospital closed its doors for the last time, with the move of wards and departments to Musgrove Park Hospital. However, in 2021 the site reopened for medical services, forming part of the Communities Families Hub.

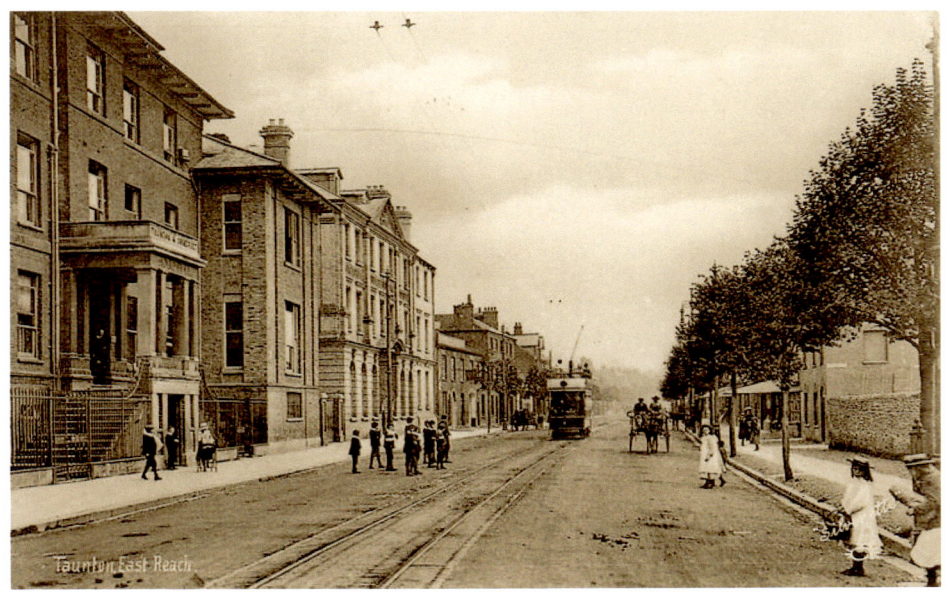

Above: East Reach with the hospital and nursing institute, pictured in the 1920s.

Below: The current medical facilities, 2022.

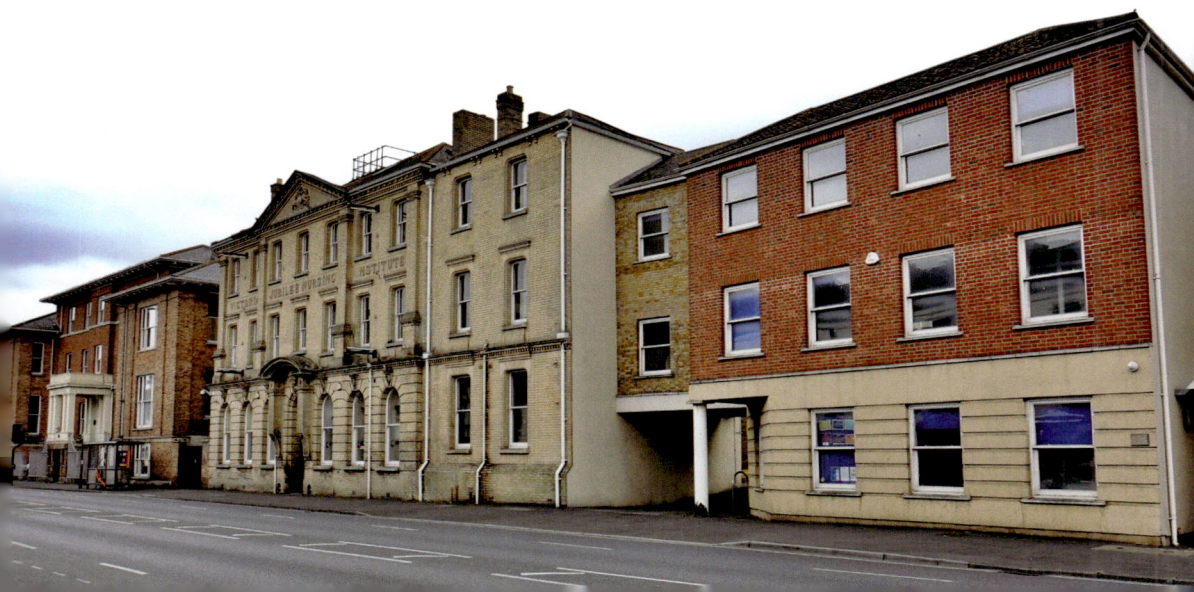

23. The Temple, 1812

The Temple Methodist Church is situated along Upper High Street, and the current building dates from 1869. The original building was funded by James Lackington (1746–1815) from the profits of his London bookshop, Temple of the Muses. The church was built in 1808 and intended for the Methodists from the Octagon, but during a disagreement with them he gave it for the use of a sect, the Kilhamites. Later, Lackington was to offer the building to the Octagon fellowship, who bought it for the sum of £1,050 and moved there in 1812.

The original building had burial grounds to both east and west sides, along with spacious vaults underneath the church. Improvements made in 1846 added a schoolroom with three classrooms in the basement and a new façade, which brought the building forward towards the street.

The congregation grew so rapidly that within twenty years more space was needed and a partial rebuild took place. Seven further classrooms and a ladies' workroom were built over the existing schoolroom. The façade was kept, as it was described as 'a fair specimen of ecclesiastical architecture' in the Gothic Revival style.

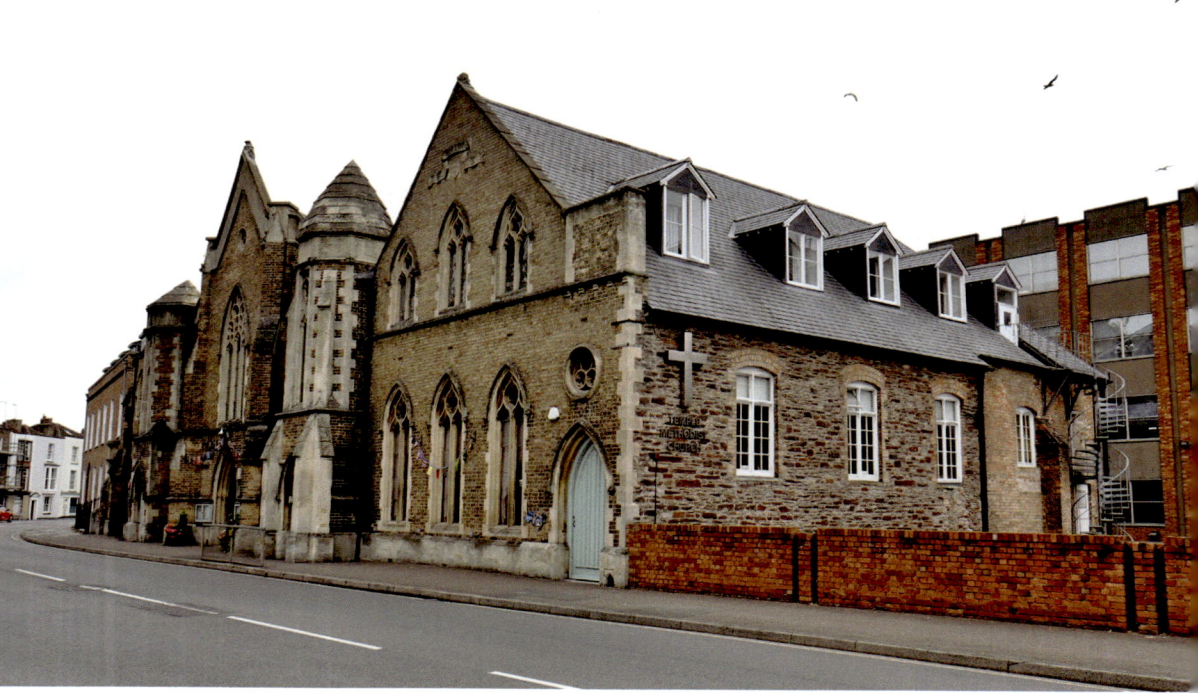

Temple Methodist Church.

24. Silver Street Baptist Church, 1815

Taunton Baptists once worshipped at what is now the Unitarian Chapel, but a group broke away and formed a church at Wellington. In 1814, a group of Particular Baptists from Wellington founded the Baptist congregation in Taunton.

The chapel on Silver Street was erected in 1815 and opened on 20 September. Galleries were added in 1824, along with a schoolroom. Numerical growth saw building development and, like many churches across the town, the schoolrooms were extended, costing £130. The foundation stone for the new rooms was laid in April 1860, and twelve Bible classrooms, an examination room and a vestry were included. Celebrations for the fiftieth anniversary of the chapel's founding took place in September 1864 after some serious repair work was carried out. Earlier in the year part of the ceiling had fallen in, damaging pews and other parts of the interior.

In 1870, architect and borough surveyor J. H. Smith was responsible for the design and re-fronted the chapel to the Italian trecento style seen today.

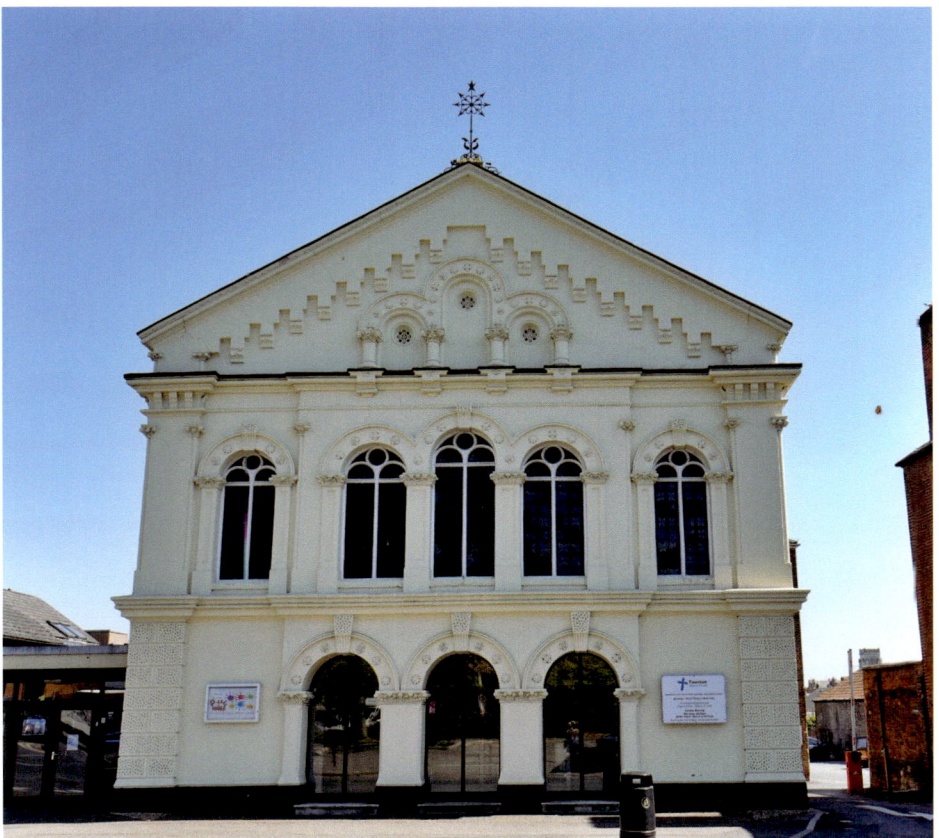

Silver Street Baptist Church's Italian trecento frontage.

25. Castle Hotel, 1816

The Castle Hotel is situated facing Castle Green. Still owned and run by the Chapman family who bought the run-down premises in 1950, it is an individual and unique hotel situated in the heart of Taunton.

The main stone front is thought to be late eighteenth century and was altered around 1816 as a private house for the Easton family. Early maps show it adjoining another property that fronted onto North Street (The Castle Inn) and included the ruined east gate (Castle Bow). By 1832 the house was the property of Mr Robert Mattock.

In 1850, Mattock offered the hotel to a former barmaid, Charlotte Clarke, who by 1866 had raised sufficient funds to buy the hotel. Trading as Clarke's Hotel until 1928, an additional storey was added and it was renamed Castle Hotel.

Goldsworthy recalls that whilst run by the Misses Sweet there was a central gallery from which you could hear the shouts of the ostlers in the yard, and the uniform of the postboys was yellow jackets, buckskin breeches and boots.

The Castle Inn was run by Mr Pattison, while hotel proprietors have been Giles, George Rawle and Charles Nation. Nation took over in around 1885 but went bankrupt in 1901. In an 1893 advert that appeared in *Industrial Great Britain*

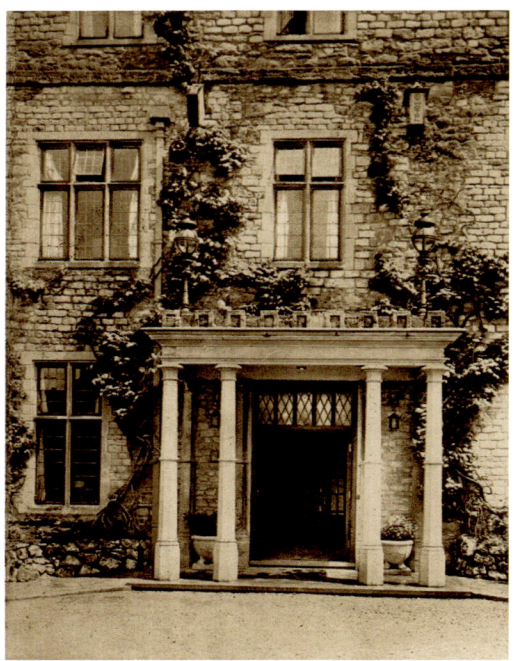

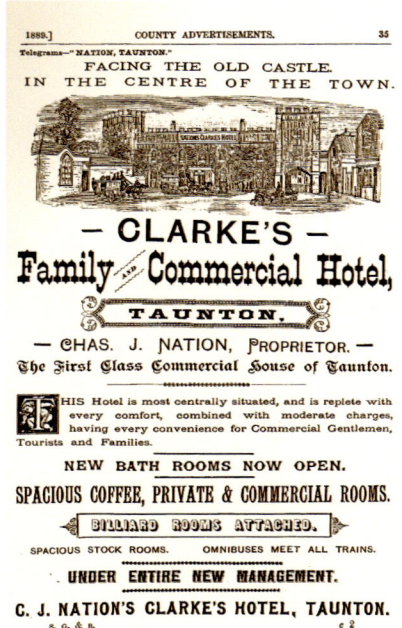

Above left: Post-1928 image of the grand front entrance.

Above right: Clarke's Hotel advertisement from 1889 – after Charles Nation became proprietor. (Courtesy of Goodman)

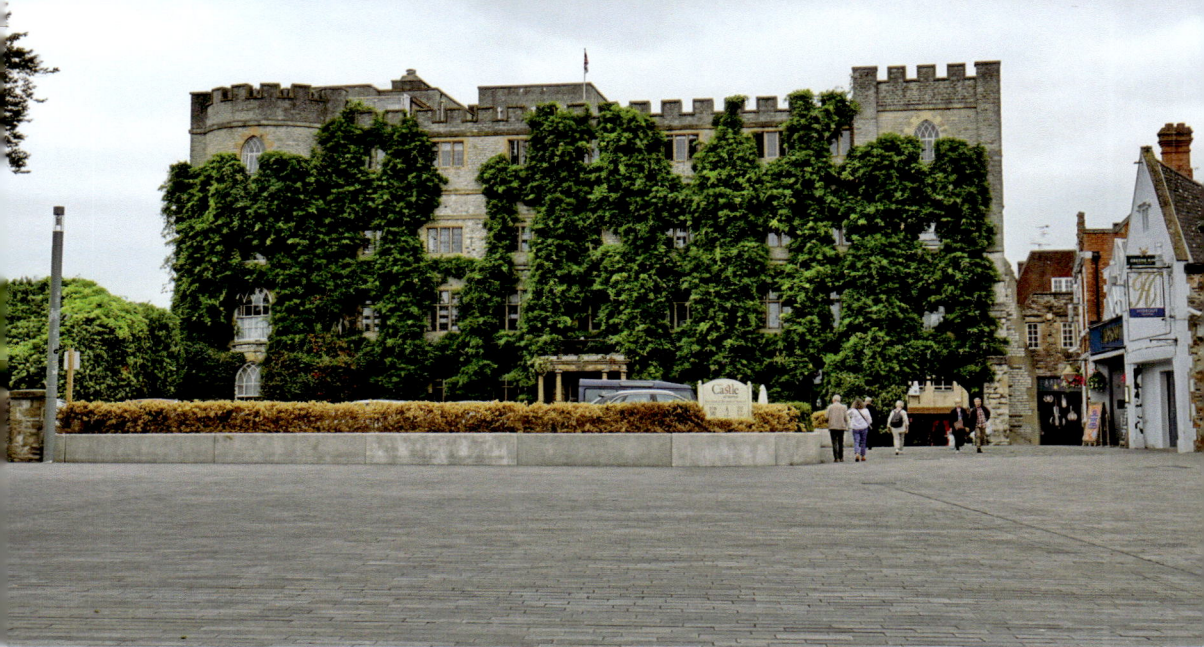

The Castle Hotel, taken from the former cattle market, now Castle Green.

mentioned Nation had been the proprietor of the hotel for seven years, yet the hotel had been in business for over 100. Its two entrances – one on North Street, the other on Castle Green – made its situation ideal for the travelling tradesman, especially with the stabling for 100 horses and their carriages.

In 1902, Harrison's Hotels took over and made extensive renovations, opening to the public in 1903 with a billiard match in new billiard rooms. Harrison's were running both the hotel and inn at this time. In 1927, Harrison's sold the inn buildings to Burton's, but they only wanted the corner plot fronting North Street (now FatFace). Mr Spiller bought the remaining portion and totally refurbished the interior, adding a floor and keeping the original frontage. Mr Spiller died in 1955 and in 1959 the new company Castle Hotel (Taunton) Ltd was formed, the hotel being under the management of Mr P. Chapman.

26. St George's Chapel (then Masonic Hall), 1821

This former Roman Catholic Church, St George's Chapel, is situated on The Crescent and was built in 1821. In 1822, Savage notes that the chapel was being built as 'these pages are going through the press' and that the Catholics were meeting in a private house on Canon Street for the time being. A feature of the building are the Ionic pilasters and columns, and the elegant steps leading to 'a chaste and elegant portal'. When it was opened in June 1822 there were two crosses – one at each end of the roof to indicate the sacred character of the building.

In July 1859, the Roman Catholic Church placed the building up for auction as they had moved to a new building on Billet Street. The building was used for a

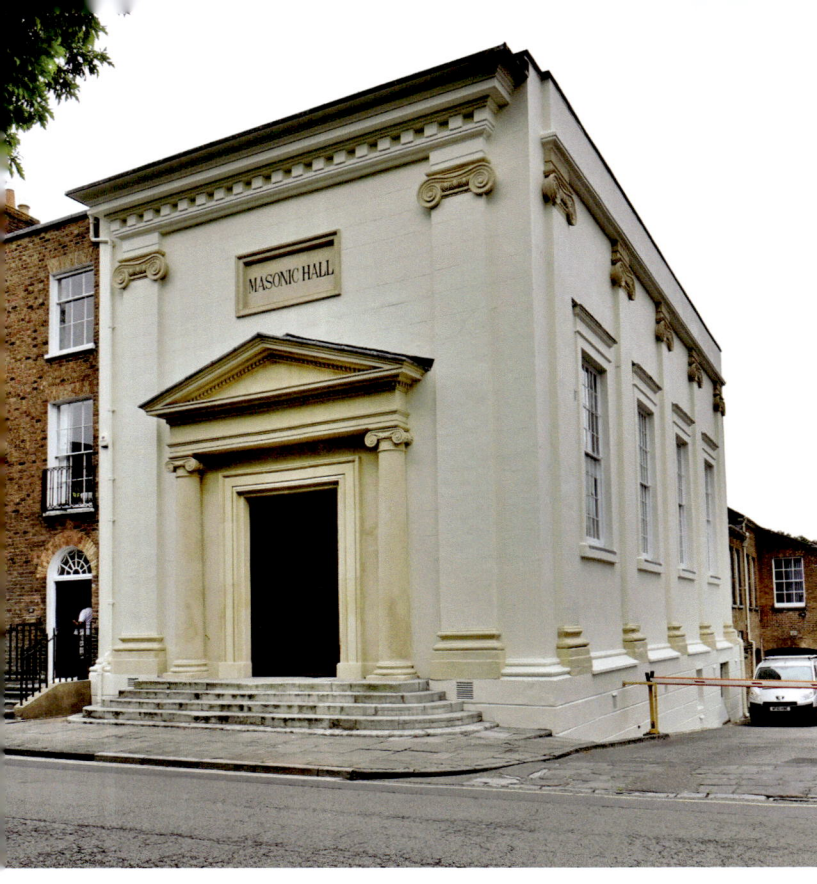

The grand front of the Masonic Hall on The Crescent.

range of purposes including as a schoolroom for girls from Huish's School and a wine cellar.

Taunton Lodge of Freemasons was founded in 1797 and purchased the premises in 1878, making necessary alterations to make it fit for their use. The first display of electric lighting in the town took place at the dedication of the Masonic Hall in 1879. Mr F. H. Varley of London lit a Serrin arc lamp which was powered by batteries. The Earl of Caernarvon performed the dedication.

A new lodge was founded in 1930 and still meets in the Masonic Hall, which hosts nine different lodges of Freemasons.

27. Firepool Lock, 1823

Firepool Lock is situated north of the River Tone and to the south of Trenchard Way (opened in 2017). It forms part of the Firepool redevelopment which aims to create both residential and leisure facilities whilst joining the railway station and town centre through walkways. The lock itself forms a junction between the Bridgwater and Taunton Canal and the River Tone.

Engineer James Hollinsworth built the lock scheme on the canal between 1823 and 1827, taking barges from Taunton to Bridgwater. Plans to join South Devon

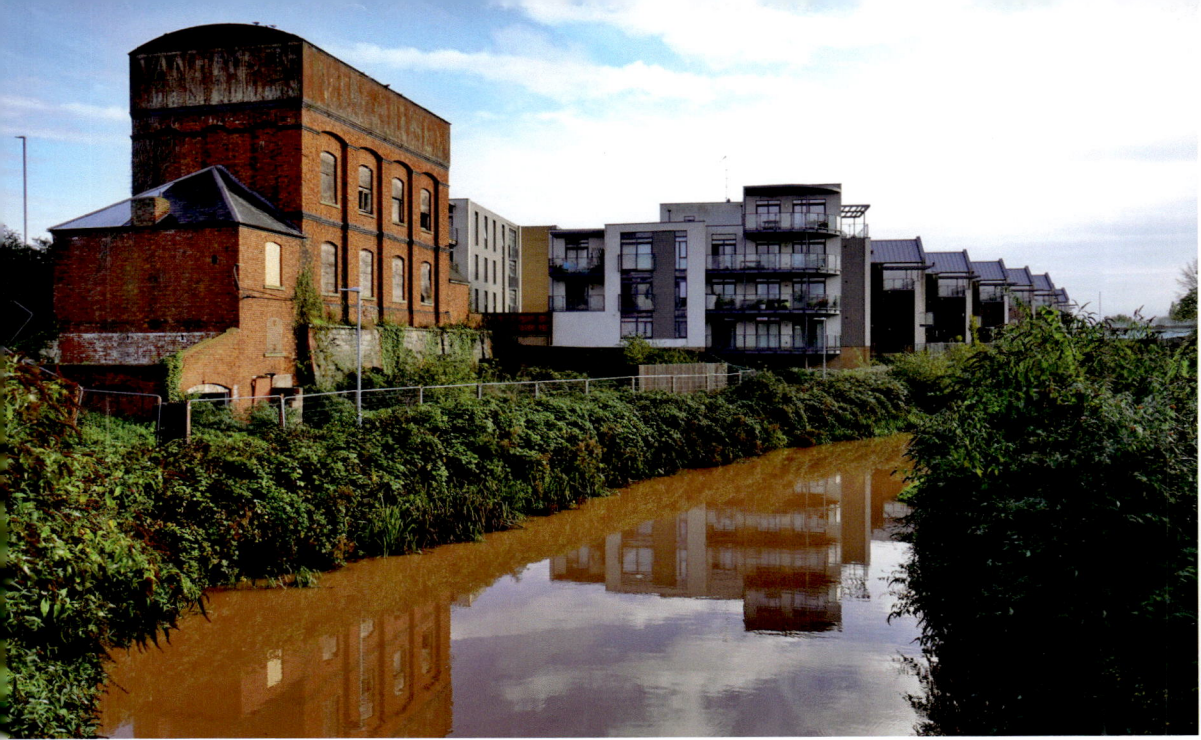

Former railway pumping station, with the Firepool development beyond.

and Bristol had been discussed for many years both before and after this canal opened, but they came to nothing. A wharf handled traffic from Huntworth, near Bridgwater, and from the Chard Canal, which connected with the Bridgwater Canal at Creech.

The lock's main function was to manage the different water level between river and canal which had a very small rise of just 1 foot. Downstream-facing gates are below the main gates to stop water flowing back into the river during dry weather or causing damage to the weir.

The River Tone was under the control of the Tone Conservators, but in 1834 the Canal Company took control. The junction with the Grand Western Canal was at Firepool and took a westerly route, eventually joining with the River Tone at French Weir. Opening in 1838, it was short-lived and was sold in 1842 as the railway arrived in town.

In 1866, the Canal Company was sold to the Bristol & Exeter Railway, who merged with the Great Western Railway (GWR) two years later. A meter was installed to measure the water taken from the river by GWR, as withdrawing too much water caused issues with the local sanitary authority.

Commercial traffic on the canal stopped around 1907, but maintenance continued as the water was fed to Bridgwater Docks, keeping it free of silt. The lock gates and paving were renewed during the 1990s.

During the Second World War the canal formed part of the Taunton Stop Line, a defensive military system aimed to stop any enemy advance by land from the west.

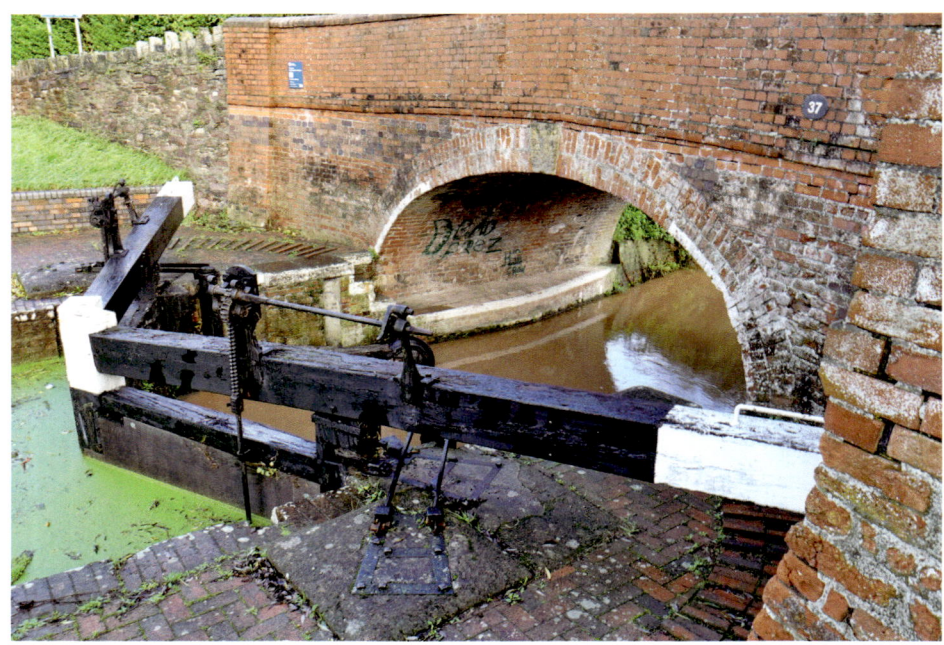

Above: The lock gates and canal bridge date to 1827.

Below: Firepool Lock, the only remaining canal lock in Taunton.

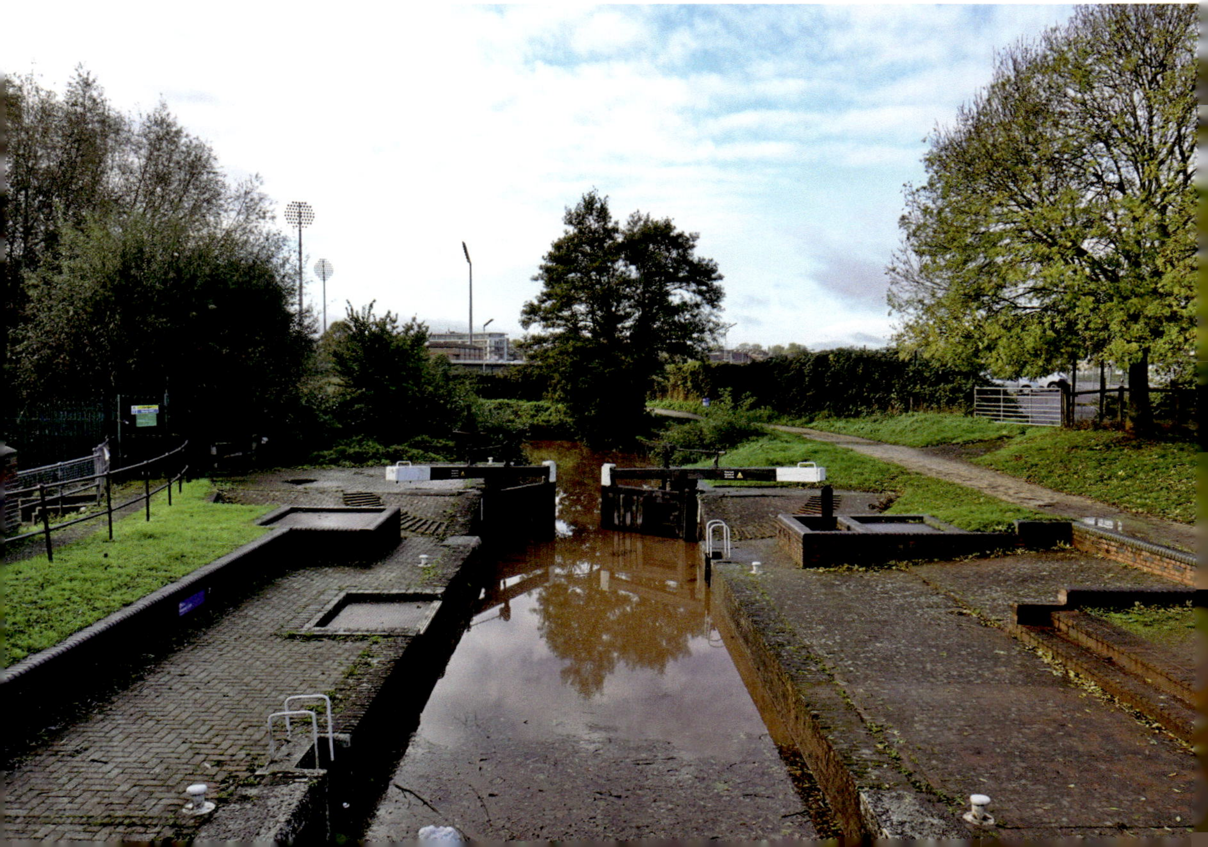

28. West Somerset Savings Bank, 1831

Situated at No. 1 Upper High Street, the former West Somerset Savings Bank was adapted from the former Full Moon Inn during 1830/31 by architect Richard Carver.

The bank was established in July 1817 by a large number of trustees who had to invest £5, and managers who had to invest £2. The first premises were on Hammet Street, then on North Street. The bank was formed for the 'purpose of encouraging industrious persons to invest such sums of money as they may wish to deposit therein'. On the opening day upwards of £500 was deposited in total from servants, apprentices, small traders, artisans and children. There was an upper limit on the amount any one person could save.

In November 1829, a meeting was held to decide which premises to purchase for the use of the institution. In January 1830, it was announced that they had purchased the premises of the Full Moon Inn, which were to be altered for use by the bank. The building was to be stuccoed and have stone projections; the alterations were to be ready by Christmas. The business finally transferred to the 'new, spacious and elegant premises at the head of High Street' in March 1831. The landlord of the former inn was John Willcocks, who was in dispute with the Town Commissioners over a strip of land given to make the building square. Later, the Commissioners denied giving the land, which resulted in court hearings in Exeter, no doubt causing some delay in the alterations.

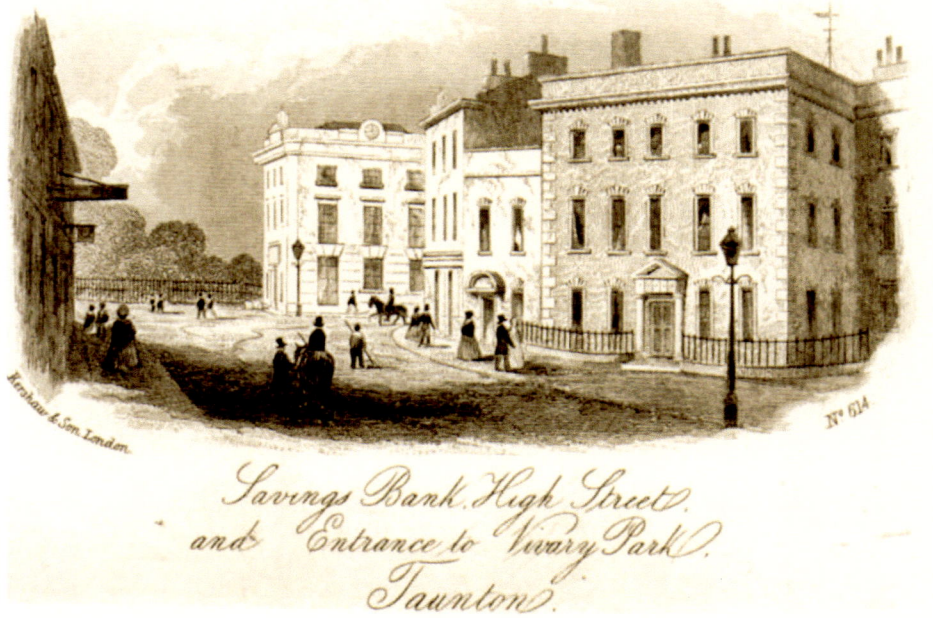

An 1850s street scene showing the Savings Bank building next to the fence for Vivary Park.

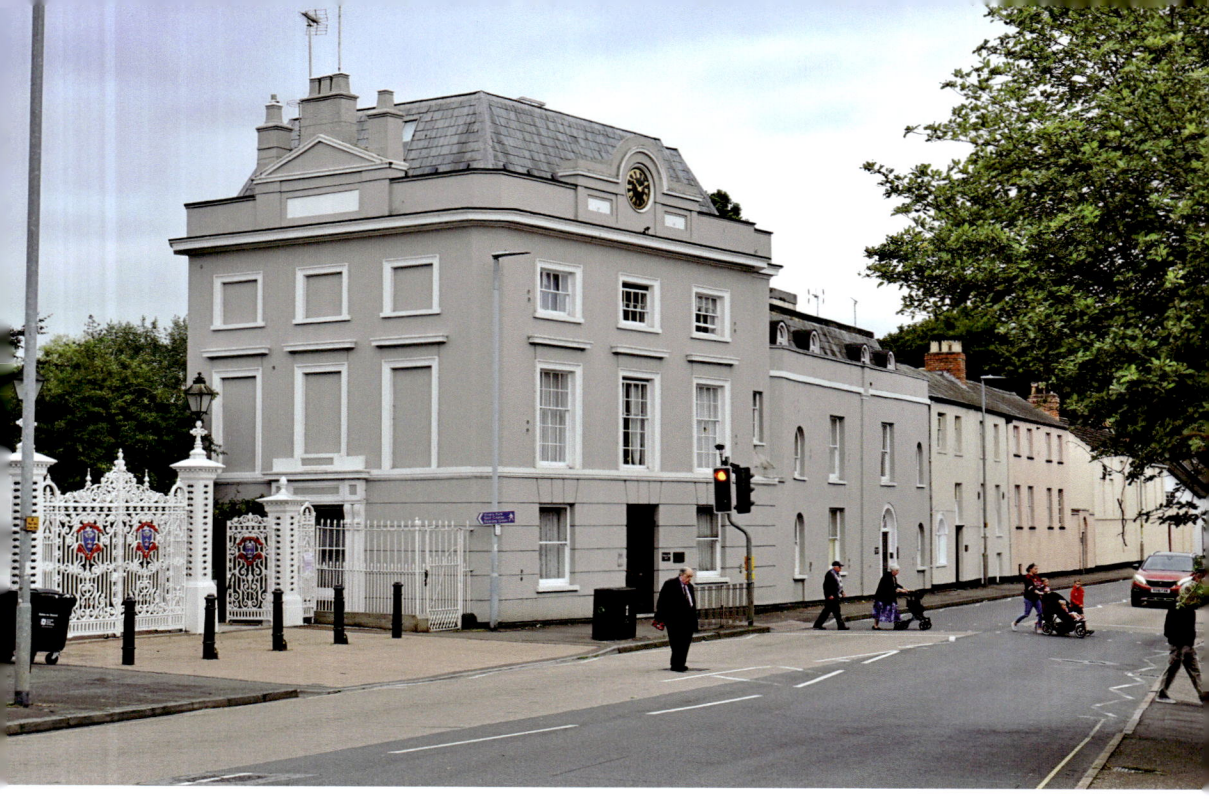

The former West Somerset Savings Bank (founded 1817) building on Upper High Street.

The building remained in use as a bank until 1987 when it was converted, along with No. 2 Upper High Street, into retirement flats.

The bank business went through a series of mergers: with Wells Savings Bank to become the Somerset Savings Bank, then Wiltshire to become the Wilts and Somerset Savings Bank. In 1888, it joined the Trustee Savings Bank (TSB) Association to offer better protection for its customers. The long history of the TSB eventually came to an end when in 1995 they merged with Lloyds Bank, but their brand continues.

29. Cheapside, 1835

Cheapside can be found in the centre of the town; it forms a small triangular island of buildings where Fore Street changes to East Street. Thought to be built around 1835, the stuccoed building is pleasantly curved on the street side, and the east end is described as having a four-storey bow. A wrought-iron balcony that was above the ground-floor window is no longer there.

In 1846, several trades within Cheapside were listed in Hunt's Directory: a wine and spirit merchant, hatmakers, a dressmaker, insurance agent, three booksellers and printers, and a boot and shoemaker. To the rear were a servant's registry office, a plumber, a painter and glazier and a hair cutter. In Goldsworthy's *Recollections*

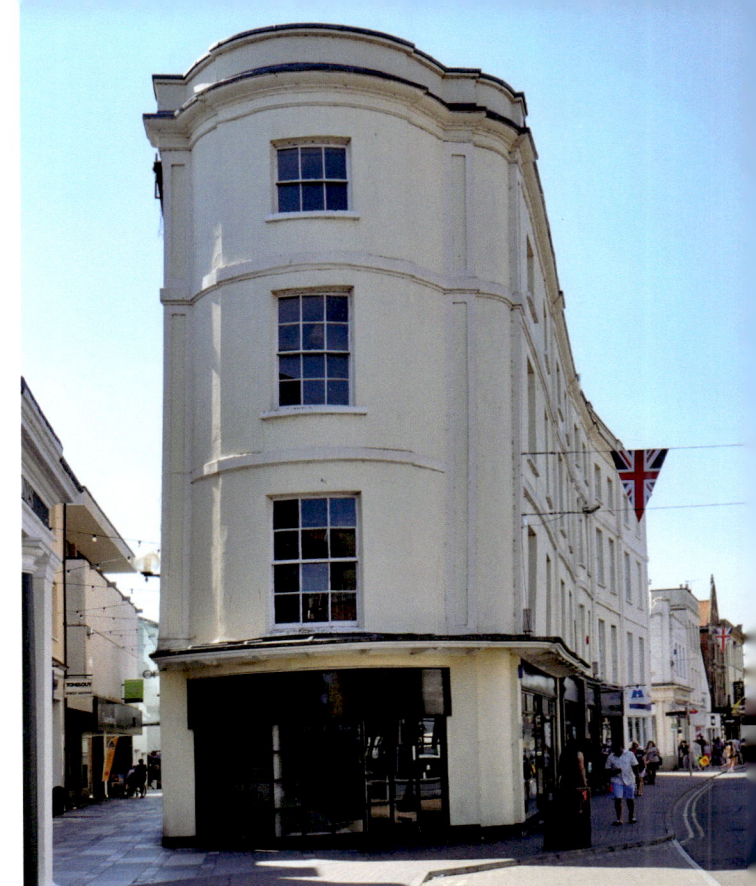

Right: The east end of Cheapside recently occupied by Deckhouse, a contemporary restaurant.

Below: Pictured from East Street looking towards the Orchard Shopping Centre.

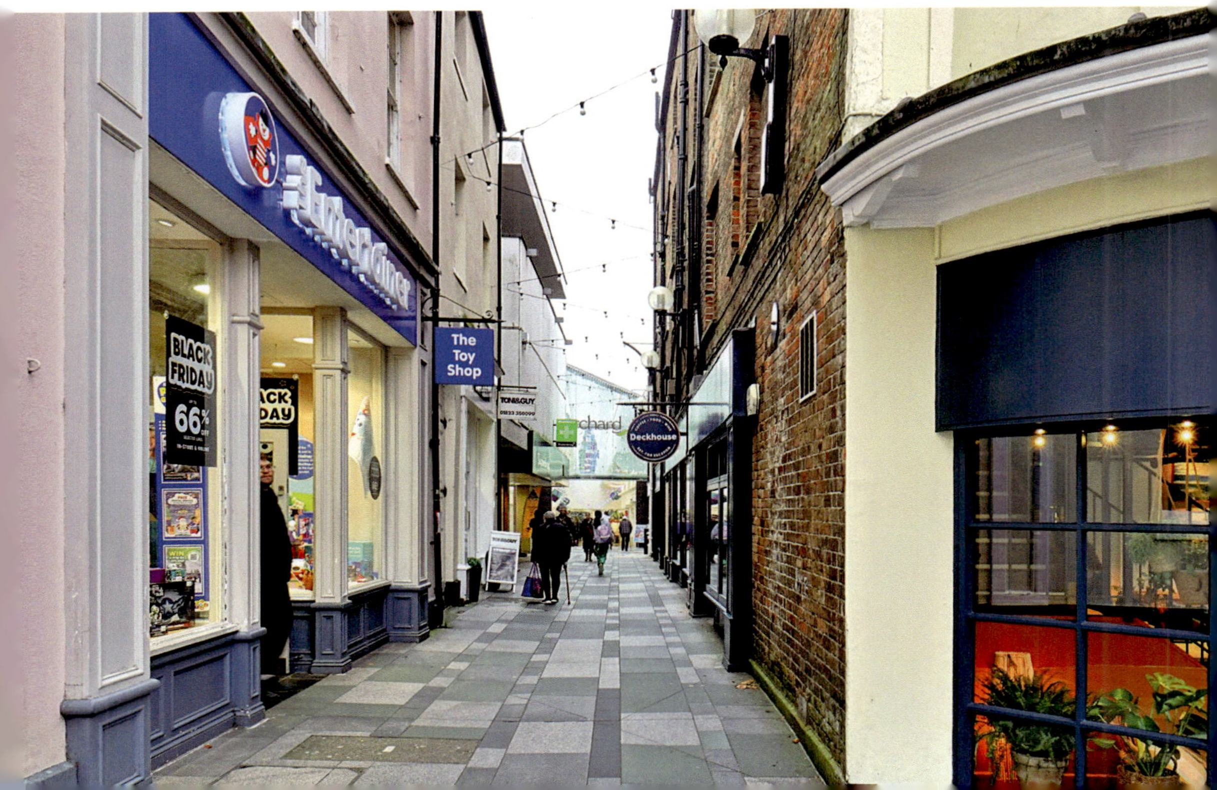

he recounts that 'there were a lot of old houses standing on the site of what is now called Cheapside'. Previously there had been a blacksmith's shop 'which was black, stinking and dirty with fires blazing, bellows blowing and the hammer and anvil going all day long' and had great trade from the nearby London Inn. Also on site was the Swan Inn and a shoemaker.

The western end of the building is occupied by Skipton Building Society and the eastern by 'Deckhouse'.

30. Railway Station, 1842

Taunton's railway station is situated along Station Road, facing Trenchard Way – the site of the goods train lines.

The first station was built in 1842 when the Bristol & Exeter line reached Taunton. Built to a design by Brunel, this was a 'one sided design' that consisted of two separate stations on the same side of the main line. One on the London side was used for Up trains. Between the platform ends the lines crossed each other to gain access to their respective platforms. At the London end they crossed again to take up their correct positions. This was an inconvenient design as, whilst it was safe for passengers with the platform on the town side of the line, it was not suitable for the trains.

Following a rapid expansion of the rail network and an amalgamation in 1868 which formed Great Western Railways, the north side buildings and three tracks between the two platforms were added. With extended and roofed platforms,

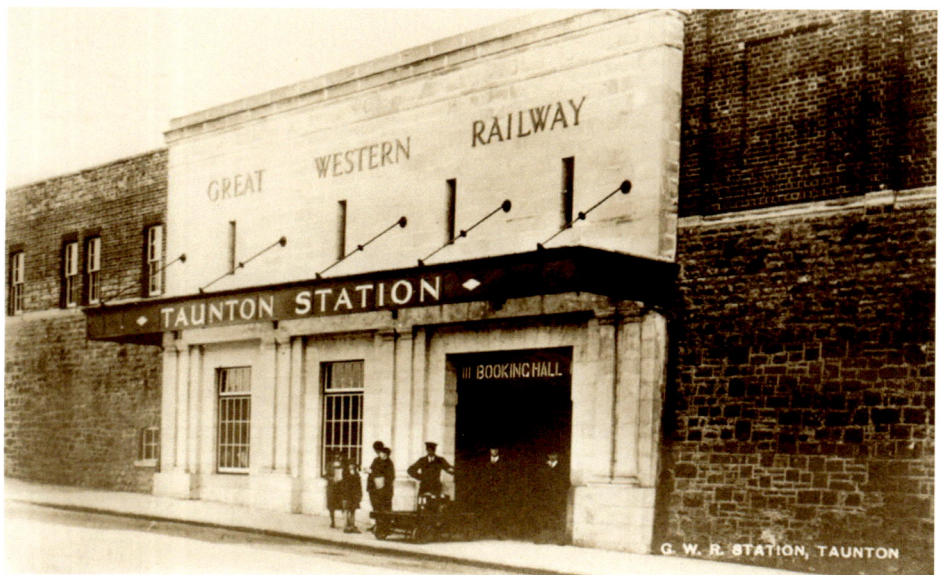

The railway station (north block) *c.* 1930, showing a newly modelled frontage.

the station began to take on a more conventional design. In 1895–96, there were further extensions to the platforms and bay platforms, a goods line to the south was added and a new engine shed was built.

The line was quadrupled in the 1930s and extensive platform remodelling took place. A subway between the two platforms was also constructed. By the end of the Second World War the station was at capacity, but by 1956 usage was in decline until the Beeching cuts really hit in the 1960s.

At its height the associated railway buildings – engineering workshops, storage, turntables, parcel depot, etc. – were extensive and situated on both sides of Station Road, along with the Great Western Hotel to the front of the south platform.

In 1983, the booking office was moved to the north side of the line, but in 2021 it was moved back to the south following modernisation of the station and parking facilities.

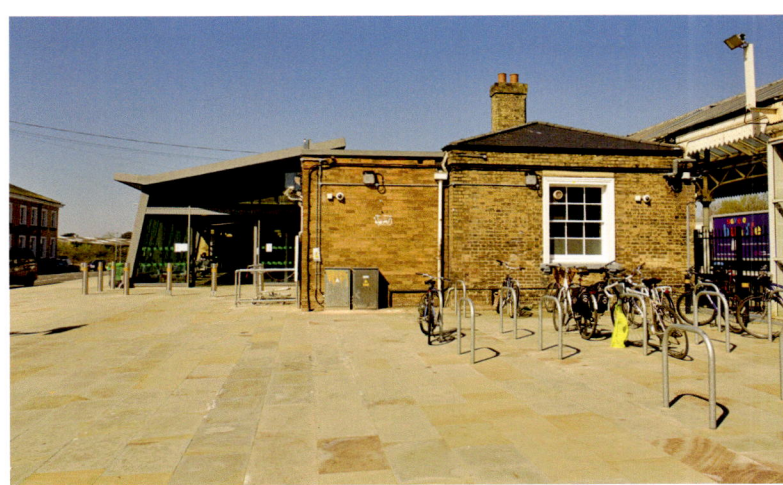

Right: The end of the south block of the station, showing the modern waiting room which was added c. 2021.

Below: South block of the railway station with the 2021 multistorey car park to the far right.

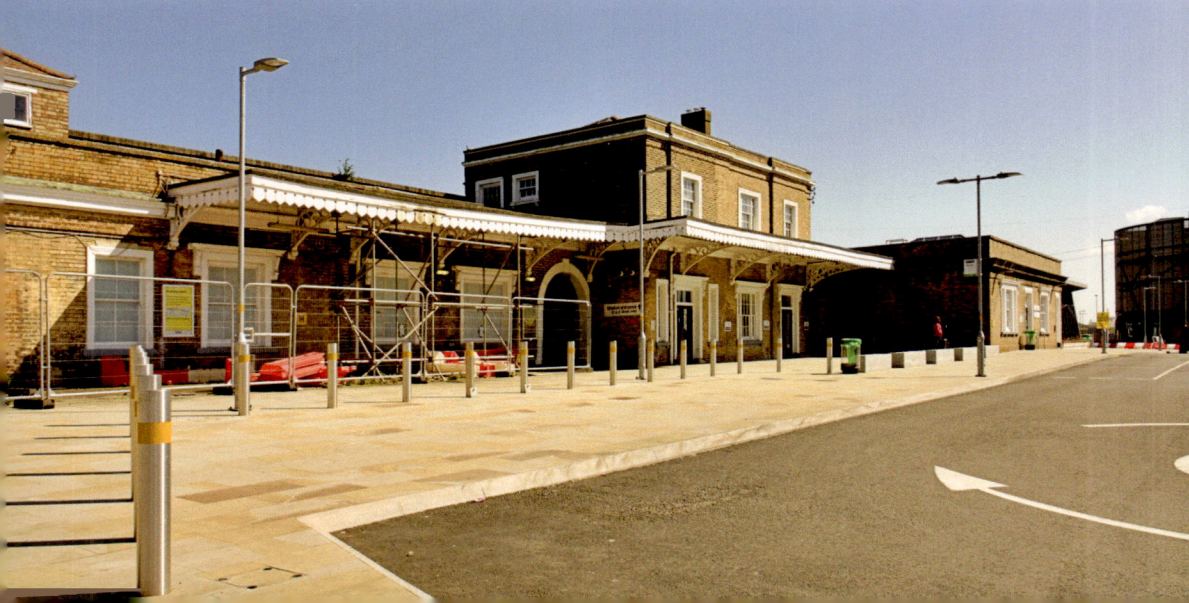

31. Holy Trinity Church, 1842

Holy Trinity Church, which describes itself as Taunton's Anglo Catholic Church, can be found on Trinity Street. The parish of Holy Trinity was formed in 1839 as the population of the district grew.

The church was consecrated on 18 June 1842 having been built to plans by Richard Carver. The tower is 90 feet high and has set-back buttresses and an openwork parapet. In December 1881, a programme of improvements was started and was completed in September 1882. The *Taunton Courier and Western Advertiser* reported on the alterations describing the exterior (unaltered) as 'structurally not one of the most pleasing of buildings to the eye'. Internal improvements consisted of adding windows to let light into the sanctuary, coloured stencilled chancel walls, encaustic tiles laid to the choir and the sanctuary (both of which had been raised by a couple of steps each). A new pulpit was made of Bath stone ornamented with carvings and a screen of the same material. The reredos (a screen or a decorated part of the wall behind an altar in a church) was embellished with a series of sacred subjects by Miss Fisher. The pews were changed for polished pitch-pine and considered to be much more comfortable than the high-backed pews they replaced. The gallery pews were to remain as box pews, and these would be free. The organ by William Hill dates to 1845; in the improvements a Mr Hill of London inspected this instrument, cleaned it and

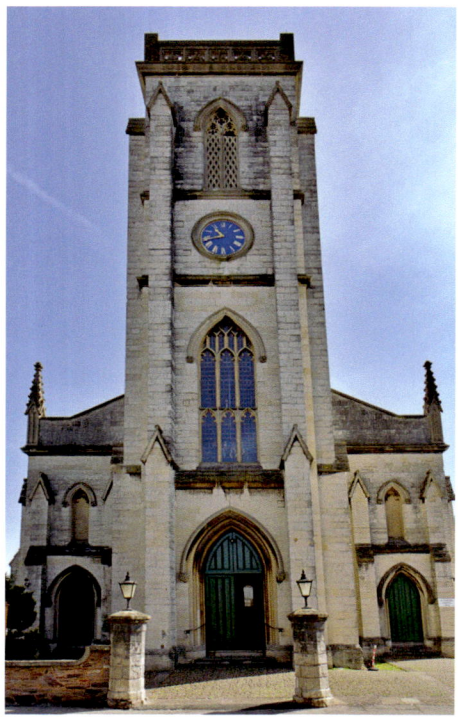

Holy Trinity Church was designed by local architect Richard Carver.

'wrought a great change'. The architect was Mr Strawbridge, builder Mr H. Spiller and cleaning, etc., by Mr Searle. The cost of all these works was £900.

In December 1885, Miss Henrietta Altham, daughter of the curate, laid the foundation stone for a parish room and schoolroom, which bore the inscription: 'This stone was laid the 3rd December 1885. William DuSautoy, vicar.' Mr Frederick Rowsell, builder of Taunton, was to undertake the work. A cavity in the stone held a bottle that contained a form of service and the names of all the 'officers' of the church. Miss Altham was presented with a silver trowel as a commemoration of her role.

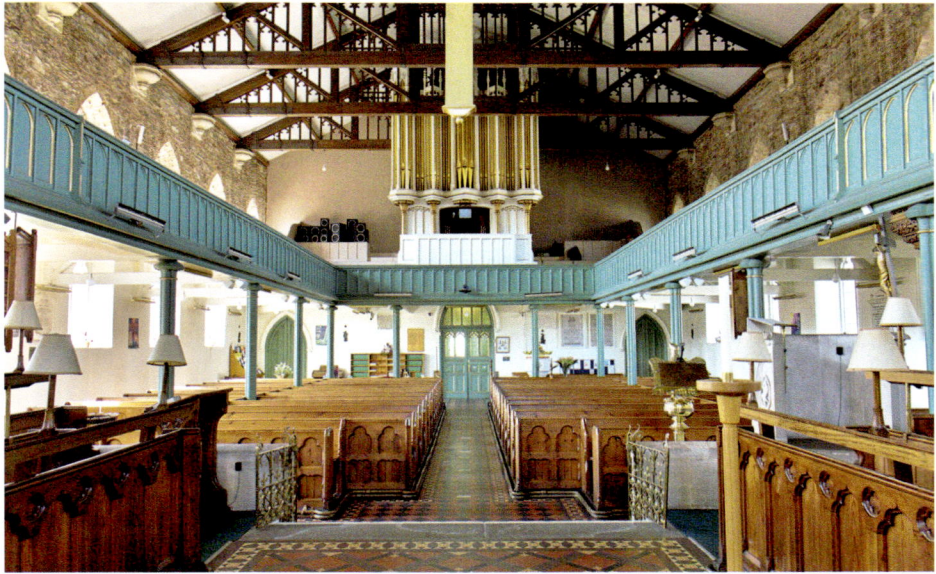

Above: Holy Trinity's interior bathed in light. The organ can be seen in the gallery.

Right: The view the visitor is greeted with on entering Holy Trinity.

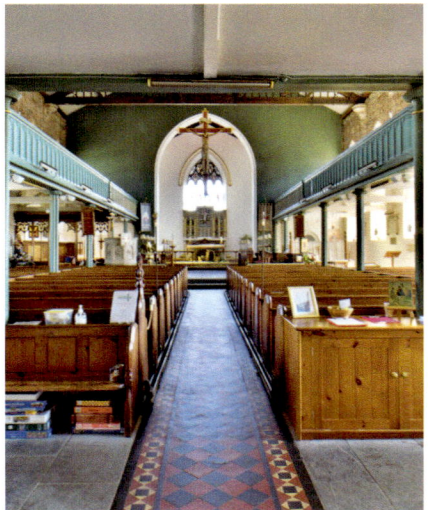

32. Queen's College, 1847

Queen's College is situated on Trull Road and was built to house the Wesleyan Collegiate Institution and Proprietary Grammar School which was founded in 1843 at the castle.

The site was developed by architect James Wilson of Bath and builder John Mason of Exeter. The large Gothic Tudor building is built in natural stone with a central tower which has a crenellated parapet and traceried bell openings. This tower held water for the college. Some internal features such as an open-well staircase with arcaded balustrade and moulded ceiling beams with a boss at the intersection points still survive. A former schoolroom is now the Great Hall.

On opening the building in 1847, the shorter name of Wesleyan Collegiate Institution was adopted. An article in *The Builder* from August 1847 stated that the 'new Wesleyan Collegiate Institution with its domestic Gothic styled frontage had been opened'. In 1888, Church of England boys were permitted admission and would attend nearby Trull Church on Sundays, whilst the Wesleyan boys continued to attend The Temple. At this point the name Queen's College was adopted. The building was changed from Grade II to Grade II* due to its historical association with the Wesleyan movement.

Neighbouring Cotlake House was acquired for junior boarders at the beginning of the twentieth century. However, by the 1930s the school was in financial trouble and taken over by a trust.

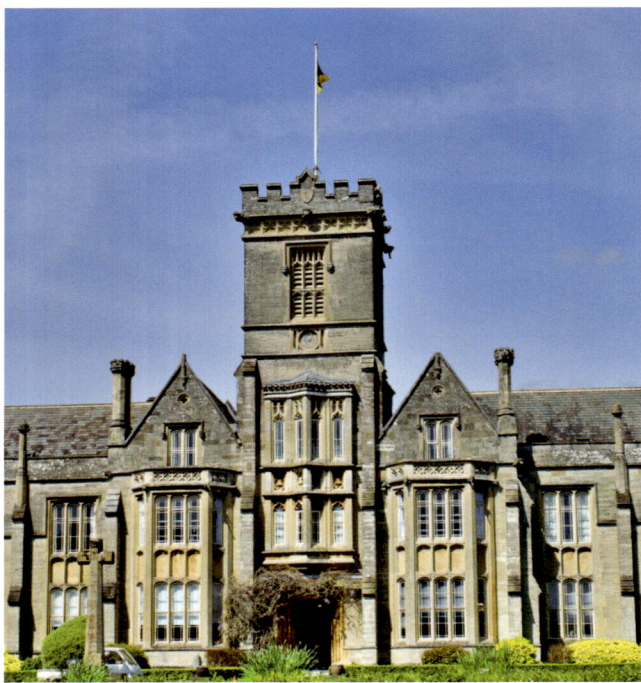

The central tower of Queen's College.

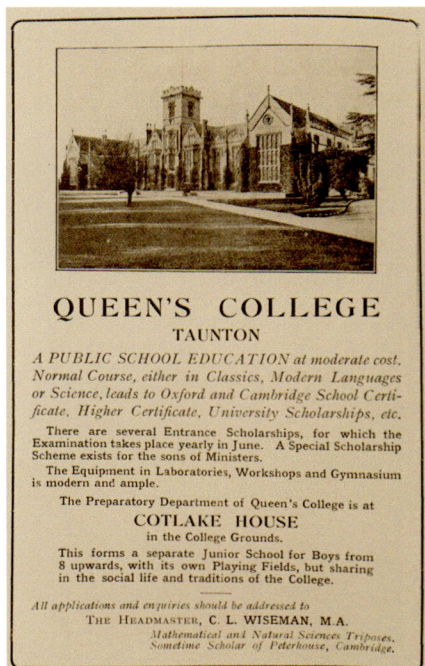

Queen's College advert from 1933. (Courtesy of Trader's Association)

In 1972, girls were admitted, and the school has continued with steady growth. Today a nursery in a newly built department, a pre-preparatory, junior and senior school form four departments across the site. A new girls' boarding wing was added in 2015, although the large majority of pupils are day pupils. Today the Methodist Independent Schools Trust runs the college.

33. Shire Hall, 1855

Shire Hall, situated on Shuttern, was built between 1855 and 1858 by architect W. B. Moffat. It was to replace the Assize Court within the castle, which was described in 1854 as 'insufficient, inconvenient, deficient and in want of repair and improvement'.

The site chosen was known as The Grove and the new building was to be fitted with a court, judges' lodgings, Clerk of the Peace's office and a record room. Richard Carver's original plans for a brick building had been rejected in favour of Moffatt's prize-winning scheme. Carver did, however, supervise the works done by Taunton builder George Pollard. Viscount Portman laid the foundation stone and the building, at a cost of £28,000, was ready to open by 1 March 1858 – in time for the Lent Assizes.

The building is Perpendicular in style and of particular note are the crenellated turrets and parapets, along with the grand entranceway with the oriel (bay)

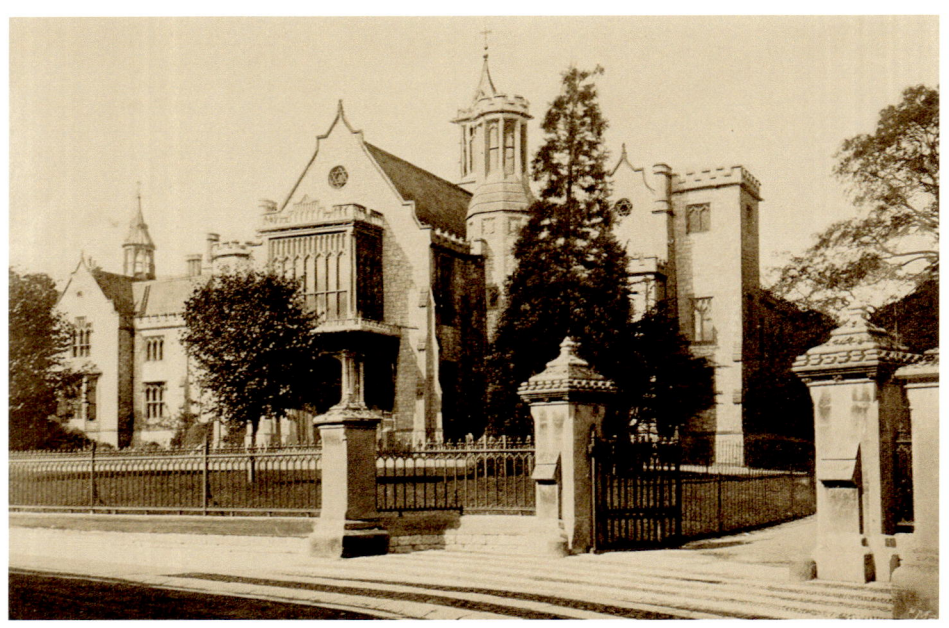

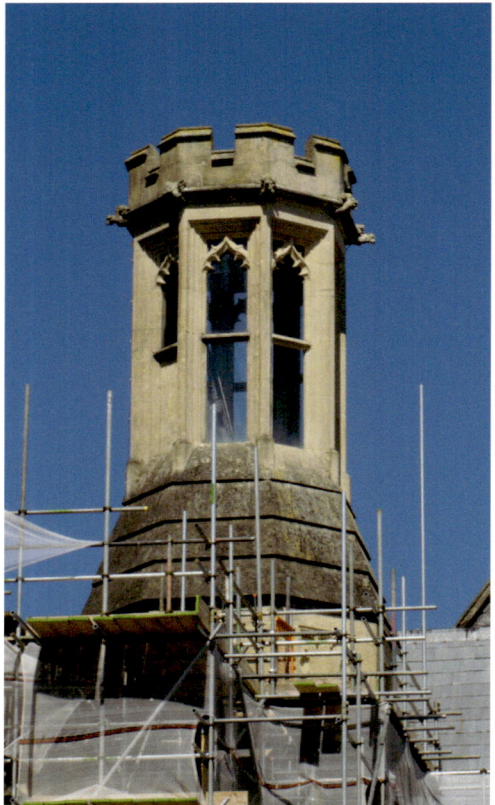

Above: Shire Hall from Shuttern before railings were removed *c.* 1909. (Courtesy of Mates)

Left: Part of one crenellated turret with gargoyles is just visible.

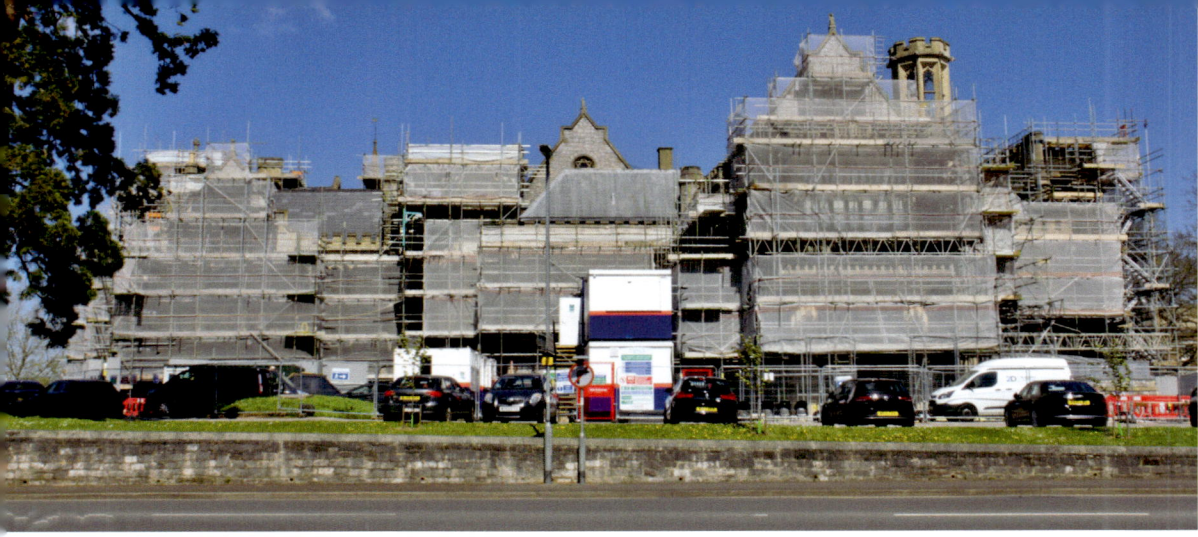

Shire Hall was shrouded in protective screening and scaffolding while much-needed renovation took place in 2022/23.

window above. The Grand Jury Room was behind this window which has a balconette from which electoral proclamations were made on occasion.

Busts within the hall were installed by Robert Arthur Kinglake, who over a number of years 'laboured to immortalize the great and good of Somerset by erecting memorial busts in the Shire Hall at Taunton'. Some of these men were Captain Robert Blake; John Locke; Richard Jefferies; Captain Speke; Henry Fielding; Colonel John Chard VC; Brigadier Gen. John Jacob, Commander of the Scinde Horse (a regiment); Dr Wilson Fox; George Williams; Charles Summers; Thomas Young; Pym; and Bishop Ken. Noted Australian female artist Miss Margaret Thomas (1842–1929), who studied under Somerset man Charles Summers, was responsible for the Fielding, Summers, Fox and Jacob busts.

Shire Hall is now the Crown, County and Family Court for Somerset.

34. St John the Evangelist Church, 1858

St John the Evangelist Church was founded by Revd F. J. Smith of Trinity Church, Taunton. It is situated on Park Street in the Tangiers district and is Grade I listed.

Noted architect George Gilbert Scott designed the building in Early English style, and the church was dedicated in 1863. It is notable as the only church in Taunton with a spire, but what catches the eye is the polychrome banded decoration of tiles (from Bridgwater). It is Scott's largely unaltered design that gives rise to the listing status. One other unique thing about this church was that its founder declared all pews were free and open to all. The usual custom was that a parishioner could pay a fee for a pew which was for their exclusive use. Those unable to afford the pew purchase fee or rent could sit in any of the free pews, usually those to the back or badly placed.

The foundation stone was laid by Master Frederick John Smith, aged ten, son of the founder, and he was presented with an engraved silver trowel to mark the occasion.

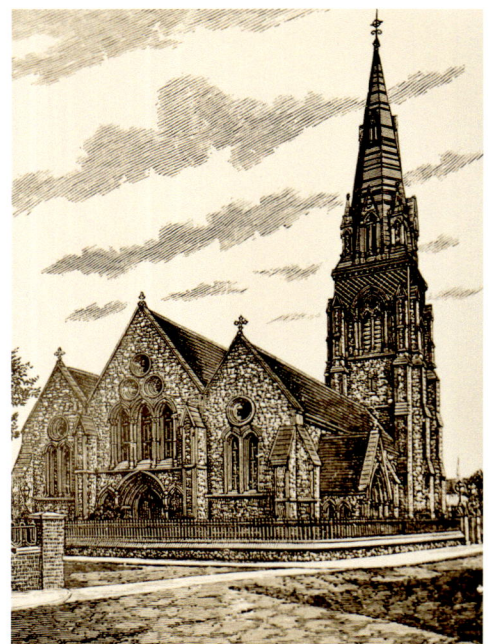
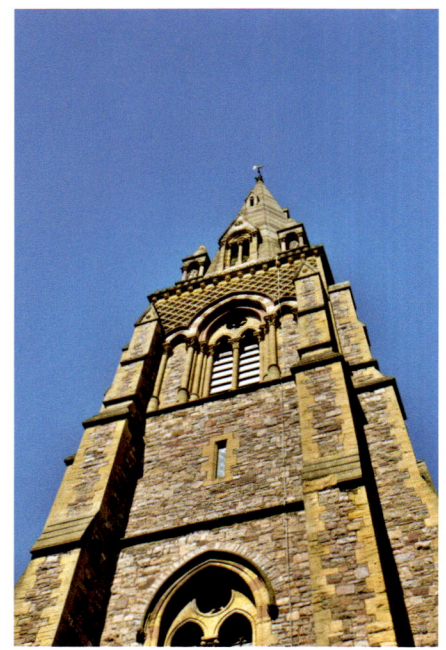
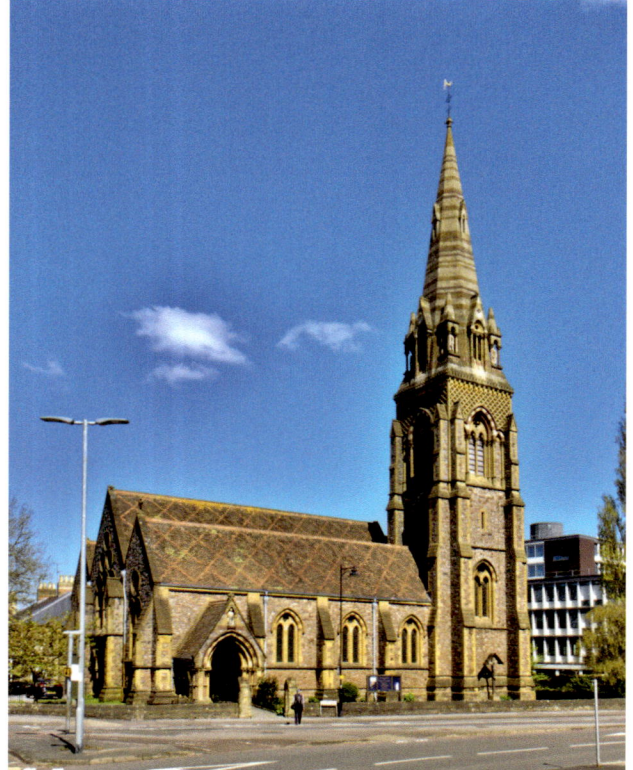

Above left: St John's, c. 1900. (Courtesy of Goodman)

Above right: The spire of St John's and the decorative stonework.

Left: A similar view of St John's today.

In October 1862 the first of the ornate carved figures (St John the Evangelist, carved by local sculptor Mr Herley who also was responsible for some of the carvings at Taunton Minster) was placed in position. The carving was 5 feet 8 inches tall. The remaining three statues were to be of three Apostles: Matthew, Mark and Luke.

In the 1890s work to adorn the chancel was undertaken by Henry Wilson, a noted Arts and Craft architect, with Charles Trask of Norton sub Hamdon making the reredos. An iron screen erected at the expense of the vicar, Revd Barrow, in memory of his mother, included representation of the animals journeying to Noah's Ark.

35. Roman Catholic Church of St George, 1860

The Catholic congregation of St George was originally based on The Crescent in the building that is now the Masonic Hall. In 1858, land was bought on Billet Street by the Franciscan nuns for the purpose of building a larger church, the congregation having outgrown their premises under the ministry of Canon Mitchell. Benjamin Bucknall was the architect and John Spiller of Taunton the builder. On 19 August 1858 the foundation stone was laid by the Hon. Right Revd Dr Clifford of Clifton and Ugbrook, and the church was opened by the

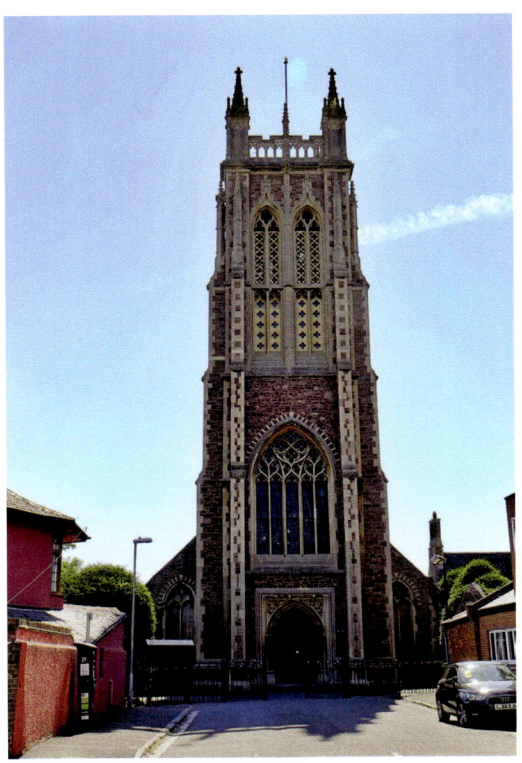

St George's, photographed from Billet Street.

Bishop of Plymouth two years later on 24 April 1860. For various reasons, the church was not consecrated until 23 April 1912.

The church is built in an early fourteenth-century style from Monkton stone rubble with Bath stone dressings. The interior includes a chancel, nave with aisles, sanctuary with side chapels, and a sacristy (a room in a church where sacred vessels and vestments are kept or meetings are held). The tower was planned to have a spire, but this wasn't built and the tower was only finished in 1873. The sacristy and a vestry provide a link to the adjoining house for the clergy. This was also designed by Bucknall and built with buff-coloured brick with patterned slate roof. Note the diagonally set chimneys.

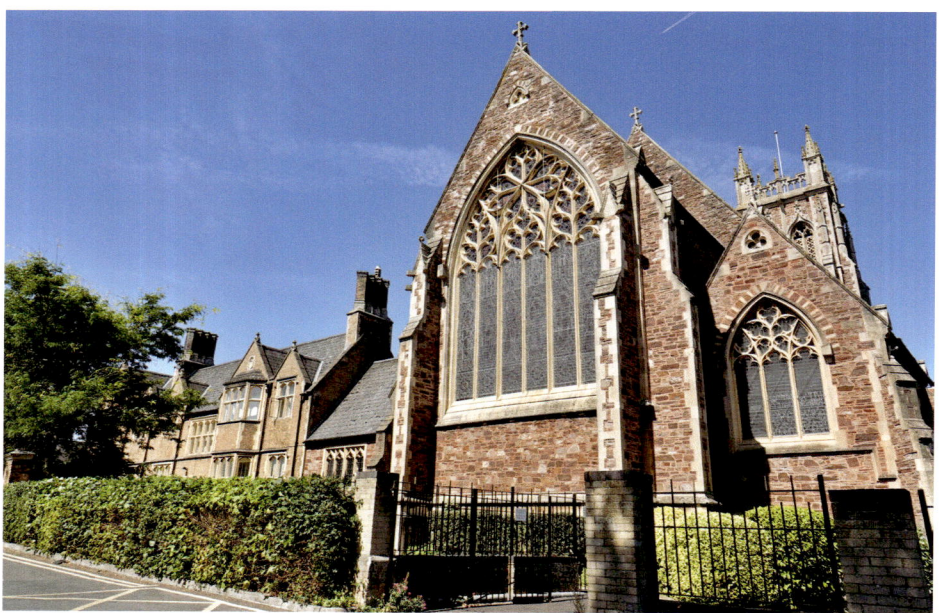

Above: St George's from the back, showing the east window of 1860 and the rectory.

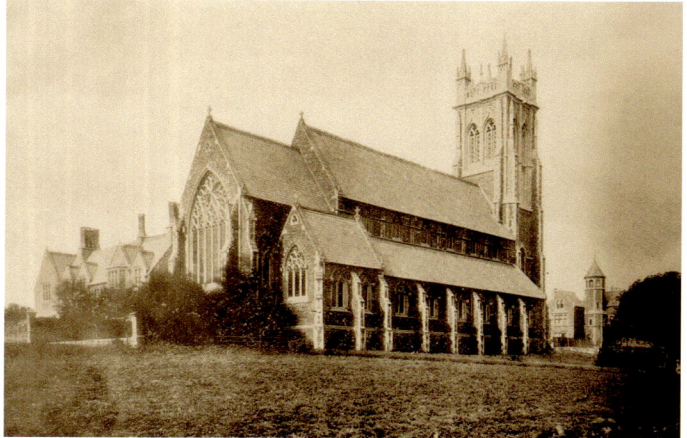

Left: St George's Church, 1933.

In 1969, major repairs included the roof being recovered with asbestos slates. The following year saw interior alterations, including a new narthex (a vestibule leading to the nave of a church) and cry room (this appears to be a quiet space for mothers to take their babies if they were crying). The 150th anniversary was commemorated in 2009 by the installation of the west window, which is by Patrick Reyntiens (1925–2021) and depicts Christ in Glory.

Since 1991 there has been a parish centre attached to the church and rectory site, which replaced a parish hall of 1933.

36. Taunton School, 1867

Taunton School was founded as the West of England Dissenters' Proprietary School in 1847. It was initially housed in four rented houses on Wellington Road, Bishops Hull. Fairwater House, Staplegrove Road, was identified as a suitable site for new buildings and was purchased in 1865. The new school was built in a Gothic style by Joseph James of London with stone from the Mendips and features a central 50-foot-tall tower. The school moved in during 1870 and became known as the Independent College.

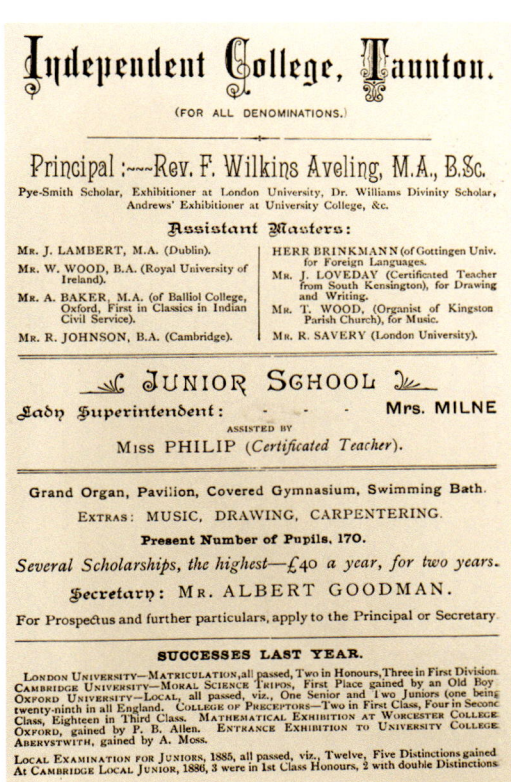

An advert from 1887 lists the principal tutors and those subjects available. (Courtesy of Goodman)

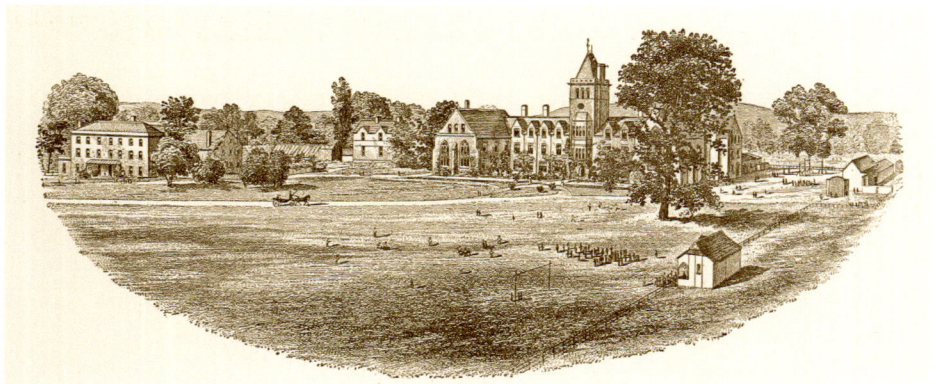

The Independent College as depicted in 1893. (Courtesy of Where to Buy)

In 1899, the name Taunton School was adopted and more buildings were added – these date from the first decade of the twentieth century. A chapel in the Early English style by Sir Frank Wills in 1906 is of particular note. A heated swimming pool, chemistry and physics labs, a reconstructed gymnasium and extended playing fields were all added during this period of growth.

As the school only accommodated boys, Weirfield School for Girls was established for the sisters of boys attending Taunton School. By 1976 the two senior schools had merged to become co-educational. The junior pupils didn't merge for several more years, although they both changed their names to Taunton Junior (Boys/Girls) School. A new purpose-built building (finished in 1995) saw the juniors become co-educational and renamed Taunton Preparatory School. These days the school has a large number of foreign pupils too, representing thirty-five different nationalities.

37. King's College, 1867

King's College was established in 1880 in an older building that was previously Taunton College and was run by Taunton College School Co. Ltd. The building, designed by C. E. Giles in a Gothic style, was erected between 1867 and 1869 by local builder Spiller of Bridge Street on the site of the former Taunton Racecourse, which closed in 1838.

Subjects taught by Taunton College included French, German, Sanskrit, music and drawing. Despite having what may be the first purpose-built science laboratory in any British school, the venture was not a success and the company was wound up in 1879. The 14-acre site was purchased by Canon Woodard in 1880 and he set up King Alfred's College for Boys.

Early struggles were overcome and at the turn of the twentieth century, development included a chapel designed by W. E. Tower, which was built over a ten-year period from 1898. In 1906, a connecting wing was added. Following the First World War part of the grounds fronting Holway Road were sold for housing and the money was used to buy 50 acres of land for playing fields.

During the twentieth century additional facilities were added: a gym, science block and a new assembly hall. Mr R. C. Unmack, headmaster from 1937 to 1965, and his

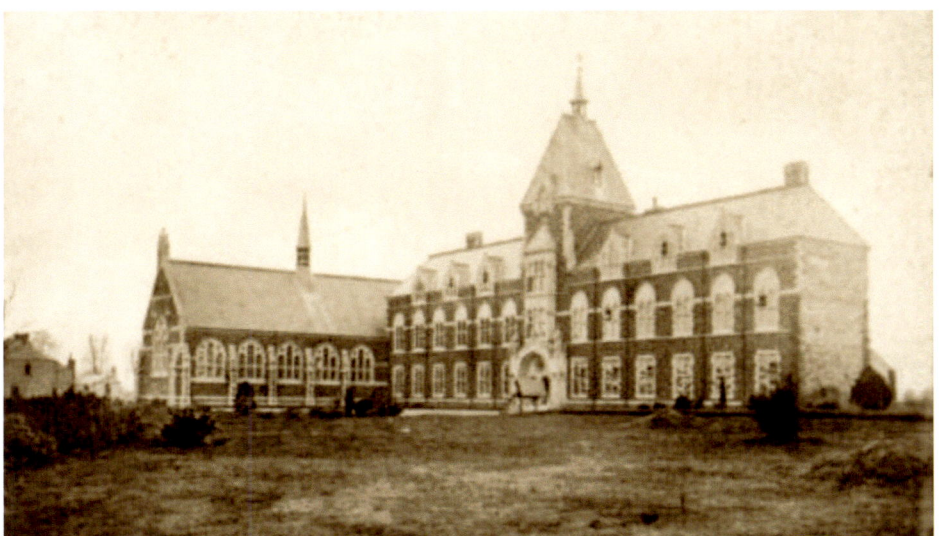

An early image of Kings College, *c.* 1876.

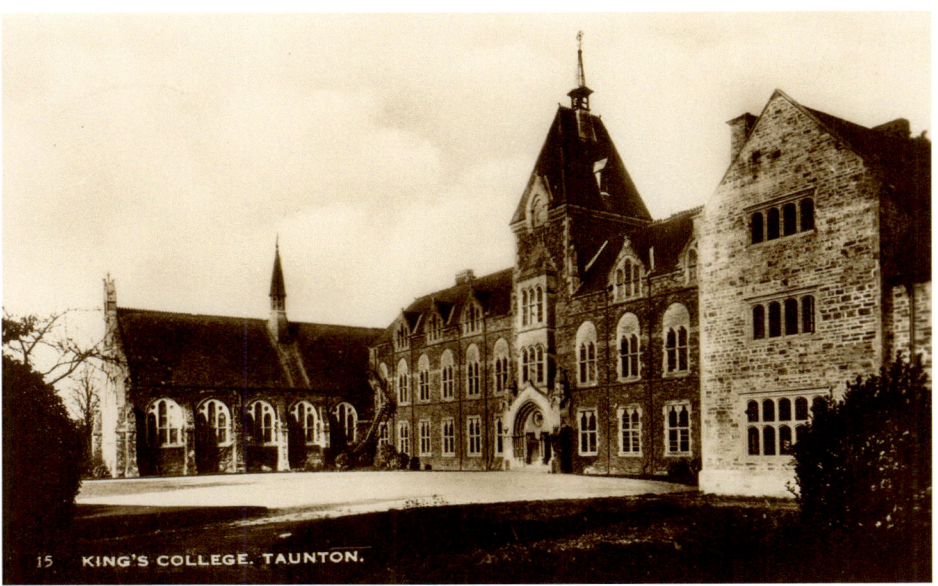

This image is undated but shows the Tudor-style house added to the right of the main building.

wife who was at one time mayor served the school for over twenty-five years. Their influence was considered an outstanding period in the history of the school.

Steady growth post-Second World War saw expansion with houses off-site being bought to accommodate pupils. In 1952, Pyrland Hall was acquired for prep boys (aged eight to thirteen). Girls were admitted to the Sixth Form in 1968, and in 1991 the school became fully co-educational.

The former convent school was bought and combined with Pyrland Hall to form King's Hall, now the boarding and day school for children aged four to thirteen.

38. The Keep, Jellalabad Barracks, 1880

The Keep, Jellalabad Barracks, forms a striking building visible from Vivary Park. Now apartments, the former entryway of the Keep can be viewed from Mount Street.

The barracks were built from 1879 to 1881 using red brick in English bond with some yellow brick. With a fortress-like appearance, this four-storey building has two projecting towers to the front and one to the rear, on what would have been the inner yard.

For several decades the Keep and the barracks formed the headquarters of District, Regular and Militia battalions, including the 3rd and 4th Battalions of the Somerset (Prince Albert's) Light Infantry, 2nd Volunteer Battalion and some of the West Somerset Yeomanry Cavalry. As the home of the county regiment, Somerset Light Infantry, it was named for one of the regiment's most famous actions: the Siege of Jellalabad, Afghanistan, 1841–42, which took place during the 1st Afghan War (1839–42). When the Somerset Light Infantry merged with

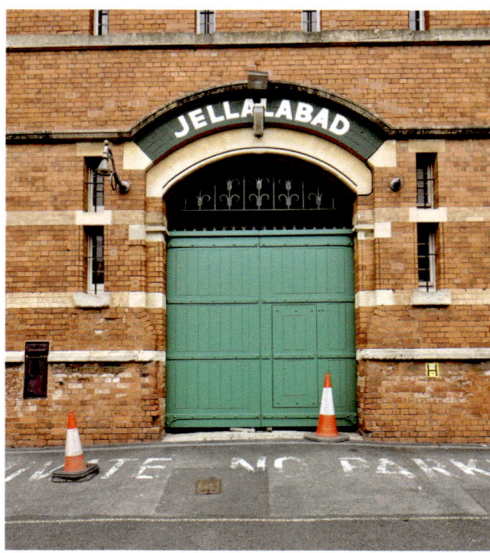

Note the purple letterbox that is marked 'Edward VII' just to the left of the entry to the Keep, Jellalabad Barracks.

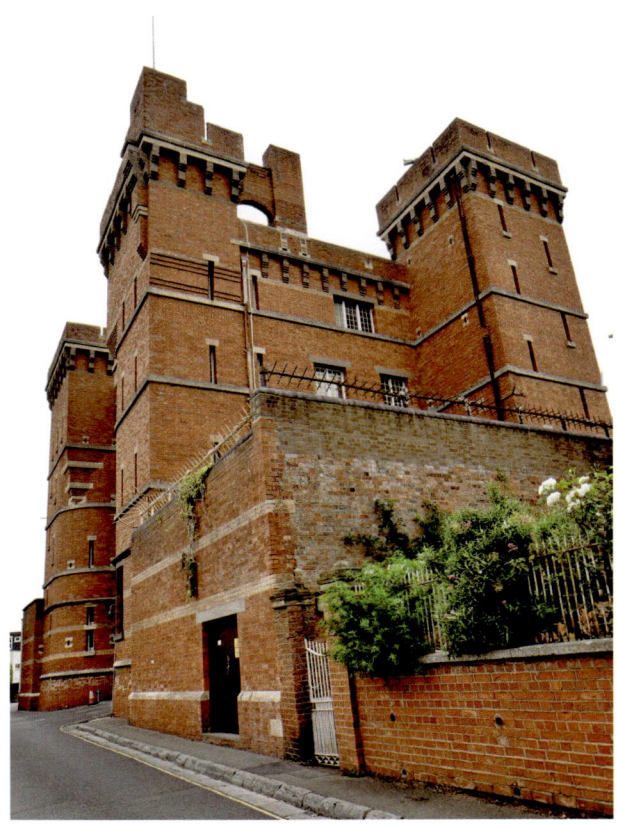

The Keep, Jellalabad Barracks, seen from Mount Street.

the Duke of Cornwall's Light Infantry to form the Somerset and Cornwall Light Infantry the regiment moved out. The Regimental Pay Office, Taunton, then used the building as their base until further army reorganisation saw the buildings sold. The County Council bought part of the redundant barracks from the army in 1962 to be used by Civil Defence HQ. It had been valued at £10,000 and alterations were estimated to be around £9,000.

In 1990, planning permission was granted to change the use of the Keep from barracks to thirty-six flats and apartments. St George's Square was the site of the former barracks and it now houses St George's Court.

39. County Ground, 1882

Cricket has been played on this site next to the River Tone since 1882. The ground is now known as the Cooper Associates County Ground, after the sponsors.

Taunton Cricket Club was formed in 1829 but had nowhere permanent to put down roots. When Taunton Athletic Club developed the now cricket ground in 1881 many local sports clubs, including rugby football, cycling, cricket and

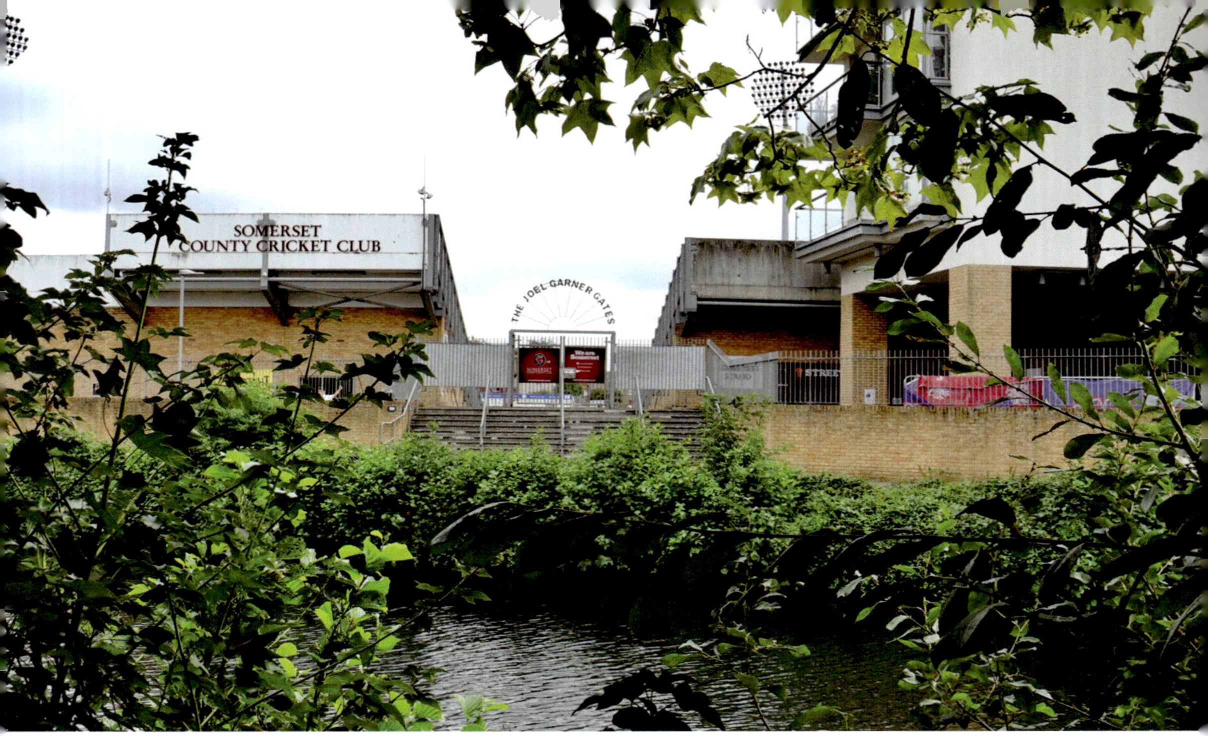

The Joel Garner Gates viewed from the other side of the River Tone.

athletics, found a home. The new ground provided a cycle track, running track and cricket pitch. Taunton Cricket Club raised funds to have a pavilion erected in around 1892, which was later known as the Old Pavilion. Taunton Cricket Club continued to use the ground until the 1970s.

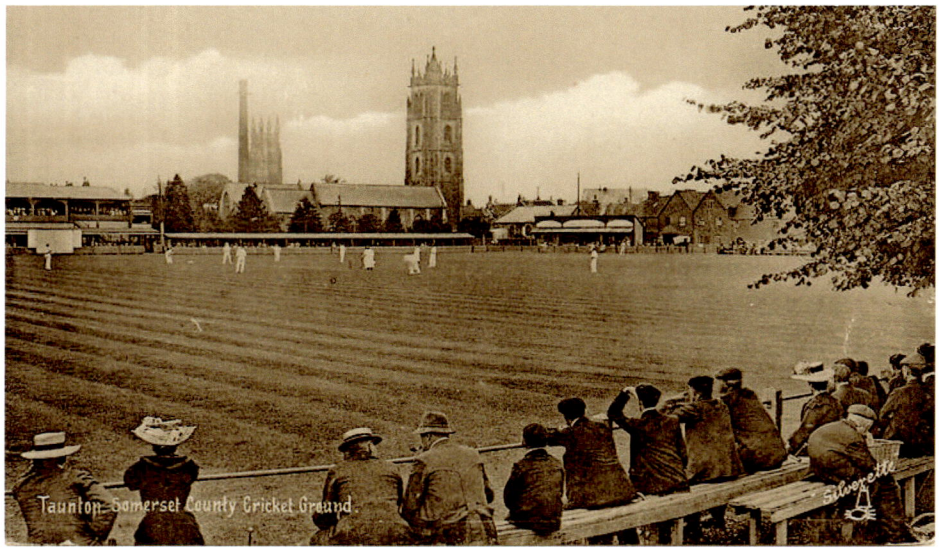

The cricket ground in the 1920s when spectators sat on the ground or wooden benches around the perimeter.

Somerset County Cricket Club leased the ground from the athletic club and bought it in 1896. *Goodman's Guide* of 1900 described the facility as being provided with a spacious and handsomely appointed pavilion, comprising a grandstand, dressing rooms, refreshment bar, etc.

Historically, the ground formed part of the medieval outlying town and adjoined the priory. At every stage of development there has been an archaeological assessment, revealing finds from prehistoric to modern times. The Somerset Cricket Museum opened in 1989 and is situated in the Old Priory Barn neighbouring the cricket ground.

Gates and stands reflect some of the great players that have been associated with the club as well as sponsors. These include gates named for Sir Vivian Richards, Joel Garner and Brian Rose, and pavilions or stands named for Sir Ian Botham, Colin Atkinson, Marcus Trescothick, Christopher Ondaatje (an investor), Harold Gimblett, James Hildreth and Andrew Caddick. The Gimblett's Hill Stand was redeveloped in spring 2022 as part of Level Playing Field, an organisation with an aim to make sports accessible and inclusive for all disabled supporters. Engraved bricks were to be reused in the new development, blending the old with the new.

With some of the country's top players, the ground continues to support all aspiring cricket players and since 2006 has been the permanent home of England women's cricket team.

Showing the 1970s Colin Atkinson Pavilion, which was redeveloped in 2010. (Courtesy of Tom Sherburn)

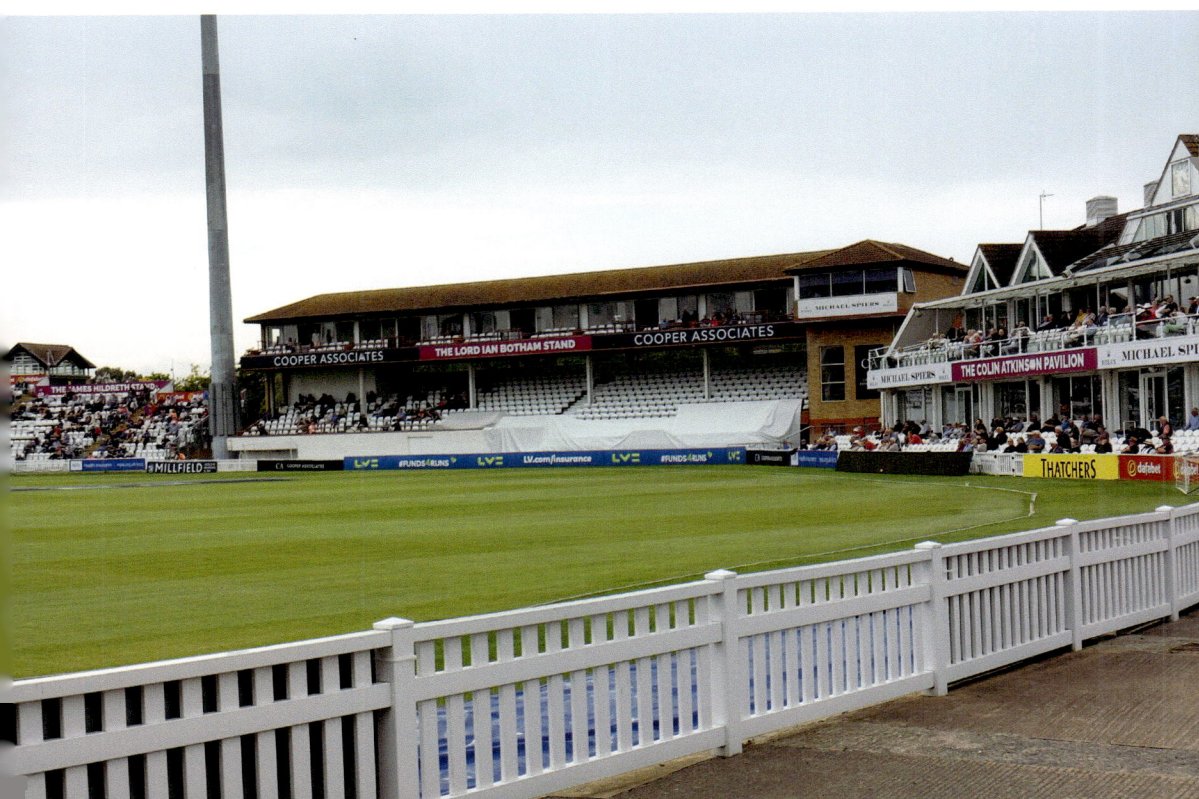

40. Collar Factory, 1888

This particular site on St Augustine Street has been chosen as representative of a major Taunton industry – that of shirt and collar making. The former factory has been remodelled as the Collar Factory, a multi-office workspace to meet the needs of twenty-first-century working post-Covid.

The factory, built on the site of what was the twelfth-century Augustinian priory, was built in red brick to plans by architect A. B. Cottam in 1899. The design was in a late Victorian Renaissance style, with twelve bays and three storeys. Internally were managers' and clerks' offices, a cutting room, a washing and starching room and an engine room. On the first floor was a machining and turning room and the second floor was for ironing and polishing. The then owner was Henry Van Trump, who went into partnership with William Henry Masding and together they created Tonevale Manufacturing Co. Ltd, which employed over 1,000 people across both Taunton and Bridgwater making shirt collars. The factory closed in 1931 and Masding moved production to Bridgwater, but Bertie Van Trump, son of Henry, bought the St Augustine Street site and went into production with Kolar Makers Ltd. Within three years the company was employing over 150 staff. As a thank you for all the hard work, excursions to the pantomime in Bristol and to the seaside at Bournemouth were organised and paid for by the company, with both attended by Van Trump.

In 1964, it was announced that the St Augustine Street factory was to close within eighteen months and the business would transfer to their extended premises in Bridgwater. Some of the staff had been with the company since its founding in 1932. One of the reasons given was the difficulty of finding girls to do the work.

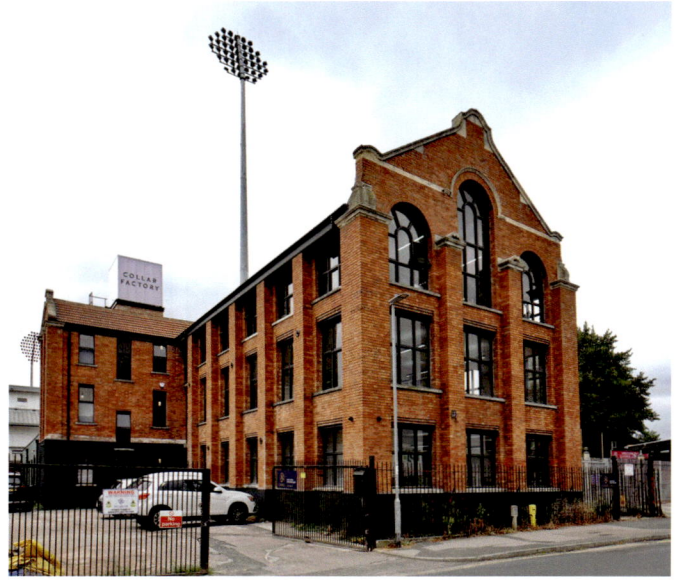

The renovated Collar Factory building on St Augustine Street.

Barnicotts Printers, who founded Taunton Wessex Press in 1800, took over the premises and used it until 2002 when the Somerset County Cricket Club bought the building. In 2017, it was sold to the current owners, Forward Space, who transformed the unit into the multi-office workspace.

41. Vivary Park, 1893

The name Vivary is taken from the Latin word *vivaria*, meaning 'a place of life', which in this case were the fish ponds of the Bishop of Winchester. During the 1970s archaeological evidence was found in the form of organic deposits, and written records indicate that the ponds supplied bream, eel and pike to the castle. A stream that runs through the grounds was a medieval leet. It was dug in 1332 and took water from the Sherford stream to drive the mill at Pool Wall and supplied the castle moat.

Prior to public ownership the park had been used by the Kinglake family to host public events, such as those held by the temperance movement, and in 1851 the newly formed Taunton Dean Horticultural and Floricultural Society held their first exhibition there.

During the 1870s it had been suggested that the park was suitable for public acquisition. Initial attempts to purchase were made in 1885/86, but objections from the park's neighbours caused Kinglake to withdraw the offer. By then the park was also being used for tennis matches, horse shows, fêtes and as part of the annual cricket festival.

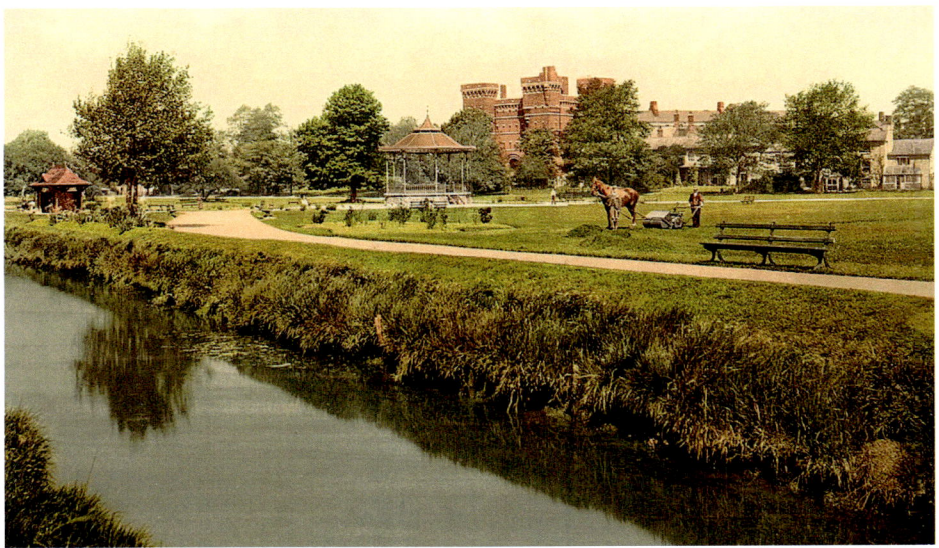

Vivary Park looking towards the Keep, *c.* 1890. Note the gardener using a horse-drawn lawn mower. (Courtesy of Detroit)

In summer 1893, a proposal for the purchase of the pleasure gardens was again raised and agreed upon. A sum of £2,000 was agreed by the council to purchase 'a close of meadow called Vivary Park', and this was conveyed to the mayor and aldermen of the borough of Taunton. Later the same year the owners of the adjoining land and tennis courts offered these up for sale to the council, who purchased them in 1894. Later additions to the park resulted in the large 19-acre park of today.

Impressive features such as the gates and bandstand were added. A fountain was bought 'off catalogue' from a Glasgow firm with funds raised in 1902 initially

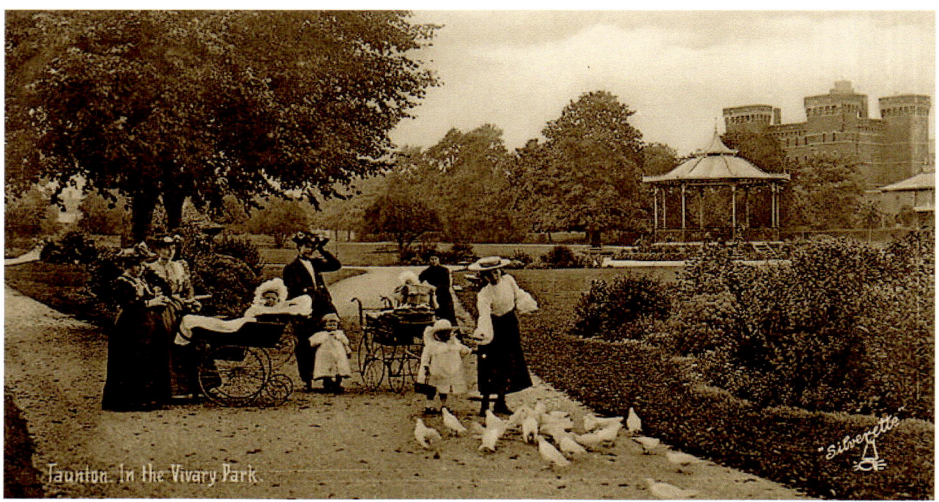

Above: A similar view of Vivary Park showing ladies walking their children and feeding the pigeons, *c*. 1920.

Below: The Grade II listed gates date to *c*. 1896, when the park was first laid out.

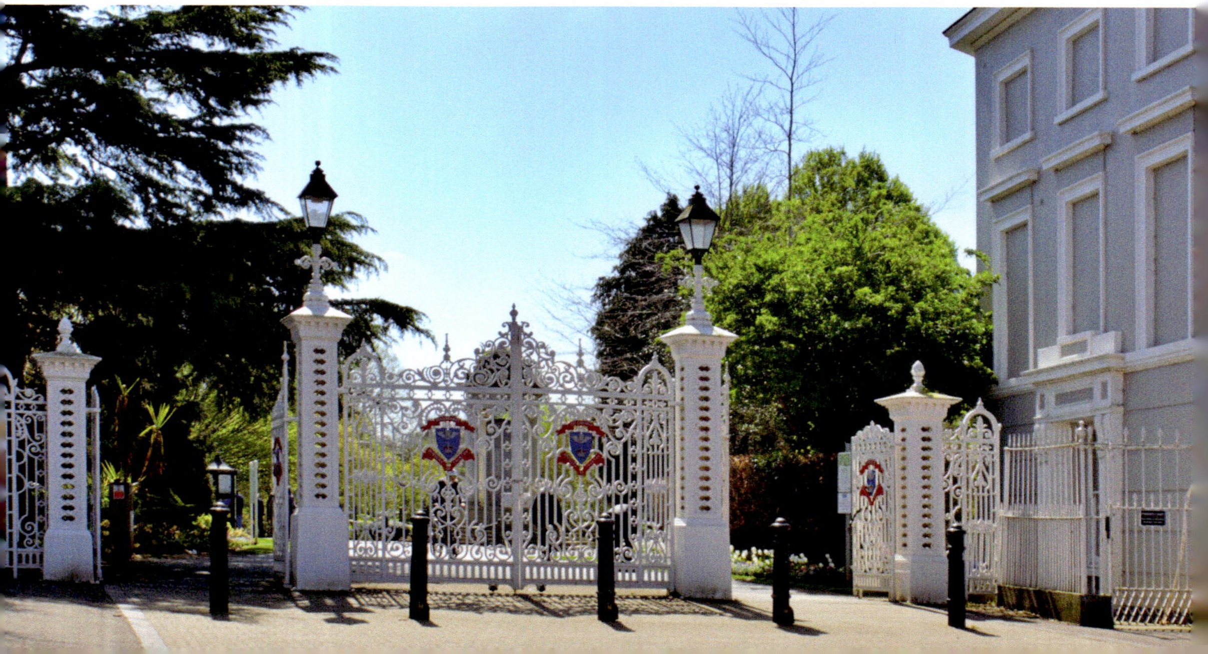

for commemorating the coronation of Edward VII but ended up commemorating Queen Victoria when it was unveiled in 1907 by the mayoress, Augusta Sibley. A war memorial was opened in 1922 and further garden landscaping took place. A golf course, a model boat pond (since 2010 a sensory garden), a model railway track and a children's playground were all added during the twentieth century.

42. Tone Bridge, 1895

The current Tone Bridge (also called 'the Bridge' or 'Town Bridge') dates from 1895 and was built using iron girders to a design by J. H. Smith. The road carried by the bridge was the main route to the north and was once the turnpike road from Hartrow to Ashill.

There may have been a ford in the vicinity before the first bridge was built and there are records of a timber bridge in 1280. A narrow masonry bridge with six arches was in place by 1570, and in 1629 there are entries in the Quarter Session records relating to the non-payment by the hundreds (districts) of Somerset towards the maintenance of the bridge. In 1635, it was reported that the 'foundation of Tone Bridge in the parish of [Taunton] St James to be in decay'.

In 1802, a man fell over the unusually low stone wall and drowned, but it wasn't until 1809 that adverts began to appear in the press for stonemasons to undertake 'building the Tone Bridge ... according to plans of the same'. This was wider and had two masonry arches. A dispute between the Commissioners of Taunton

Looking towards Tone Bridge with the cricket ground and Coal Orchard beyond.

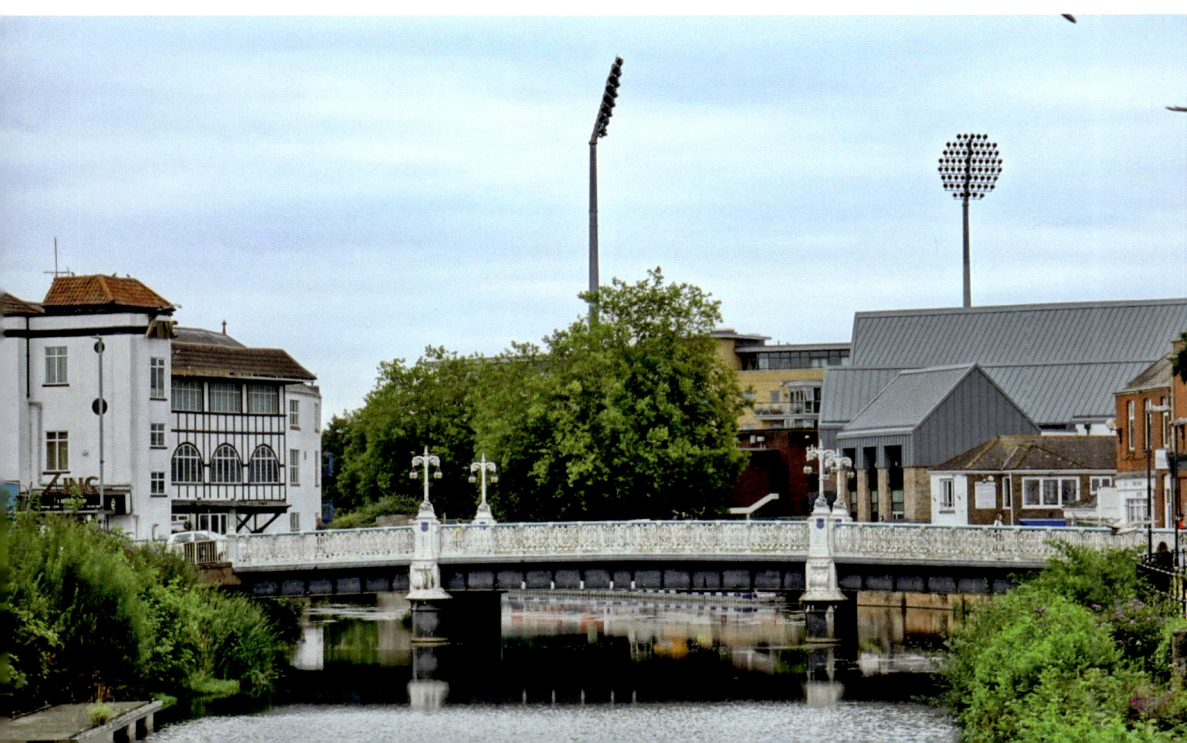

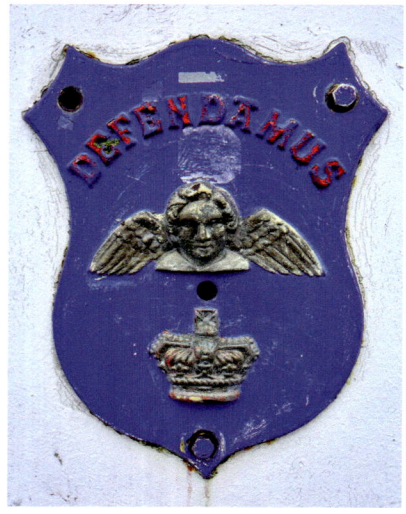

'Defendamus' (Let us Defend) appears on a plinth at the base of the lamp stands.

Bridges and the county of Somerset as to the right to repair the bridge ended up in the Court of King's Bench against the Commissioners. Harry Frier, a Victorian popular watercolour artist, depicted the bridge in around 1810 (taken from an old print) and it shows a stone-built structure with safety refuges for pedestrians.

Plans for a cast-iron bridge were made in 1828 but weren't implemented at the time. Alterations in 1834 added a larger masonry arch between the original two with the aim of improving navigation and to prevent flooding. As flood conditions worsened the need for improvement led to the bridge of today. Iron girders were replaced by steel in the 1930s, but the original lamp standards and cast-iron parapets are still in use today. The council had been running electric lights, installed by a private company, and these were reputed to be some of the first in Britain.

43. School of Art, 1905

The former Taunton School of Art is situated on Corporation Street and is now the Cosy Club. It was designed by A. Basil Cottam, a prolific Somerset architect based in Bridgwater. A striking feature of this neoclassical building is the two Ionic pillars, described by Pevsner as 'giant'.

Prior to having their own dedicated building, the Taunton School of Science and Art met at a public hall on Bath Place. It was founded on 2 June 1856 following earlier failed attempts to create arts establishments. In 1889, the school moved to the Victoria Rooms until the Corporation Street premises were opened in 1905. Two ground-floor rooms, originally for the weaving and architecture departments, were one large room by 1956.

By the mid-twentieth century the college was inhibited from some of the things it wanted to do due to lack of accommodation. At the annual summer exhibition

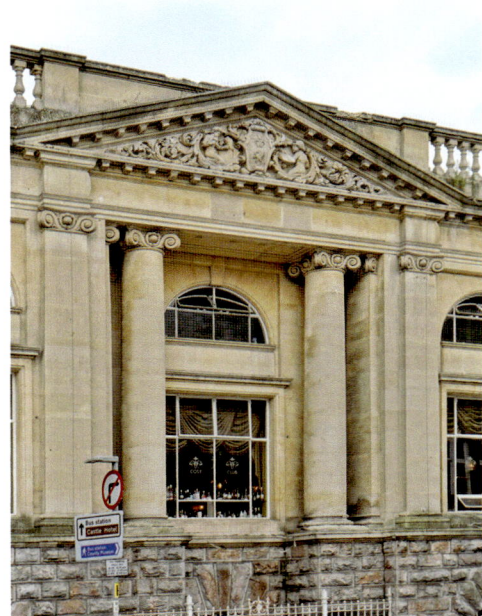

Right: The grand neoclassical frontage of the art school.

Below: Taunton Art School in 1909. (Courtesy of Mates)

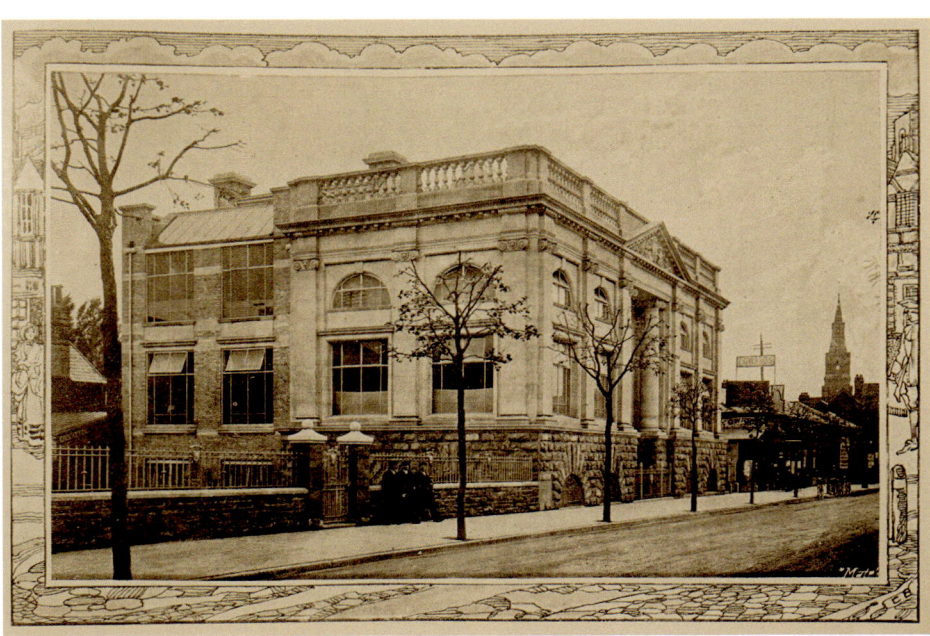

in 1950, the then principal told the press that despite this the quality of student's work was the highest standard ever. In 1959, as Somerset College of Art and Technology, the establishment moved to Wellington Road.

One of the college's alumni is West Somerset artist Rachel Reckitt (1905–98).

44. Post Office, 1911

The former post office on North Street, now home to chain restaurant Ask Italian, was opened in 1911 to a design by architect John Rutherford (Ministry of Works) and built by Bridgwater builder Pollard & Son. The site was that of the former Spread Eagle Inn, one of several inns along North Street. The new building replaced an old, outdated building on Hammet Street which was in service from the mid-nineteenth century.

The new building had two entrances with keystones that indicated the building's use. It was built in the Renaissance style with red bricks in an English bond pattern, whilst Portland stone ashlar was used for the ground floor. The brick parapet hides the roof.

Donations to fund a public clock were plentiful and the £60 needed was soon raised. The clock was erected during May 1911 and was automatically corrected to the time at Greenwich at 10 a.m. daily, meaning that those on North Street could always be sure of the correct time. Fourteen other clocks in the building were also automatically adjusted at the same time. This was the first such clock in the south-west of England. Plans were suggested to link St Mary's clock, so that when the church chimed those within hearing distance would also be sure of the correct time. Although the clock is still there and working, it is looking in a sad state of repair today.

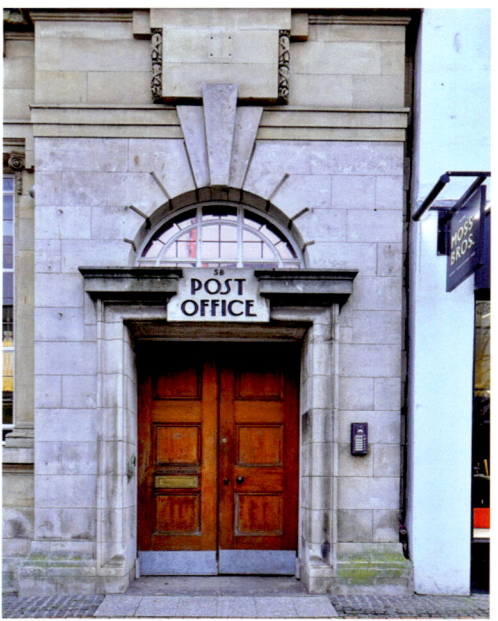 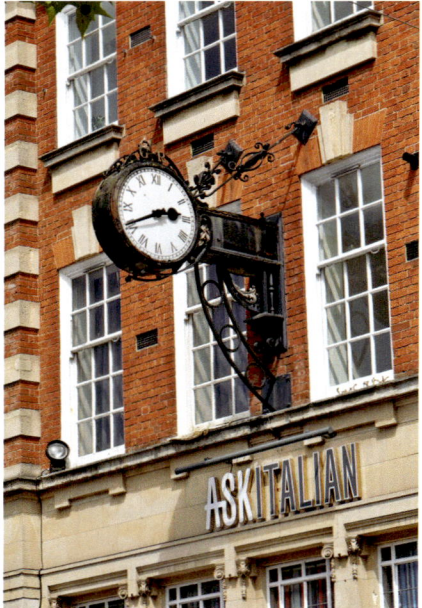

Above left: One of the two main entryways into the former post office.

Above right: The 1911 clock bears the initials 'G R' and a crown.

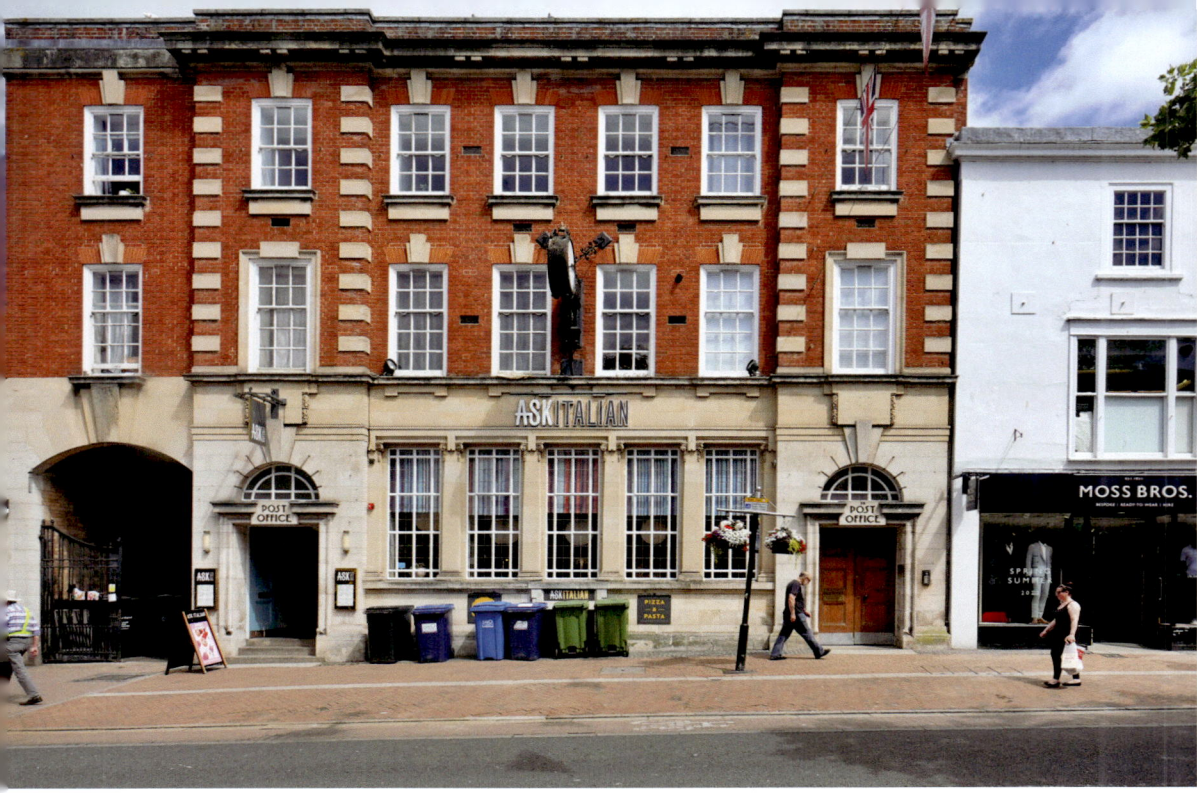

The former post office opened in 1911. It is now chain restaurant Ask Italian.

The archway gave the mail carts access to the rear yard, which was secured by iron gates. Services were offered for postage, telegrams and telephone for which 'the employment of female labour as telephone operators' was allowed for the first time. The top floor held the telegraphic equipment, which was used to send telegrams, these having been sent from customers on the ground floor by means of a pneumatic tube.

When the post office was closed down the facilities were housed inside another shop unit, the long-established County Stores. However, when this business closed in 2019 it looked like the town was going to be left without a post office until a home was found on Fore Street within WHSmiths.

45. Deller's Café, 1923

Deller's Café was part of Messr's Dellers of Exeter and Paignton and opened their Taunton café on 27 June 1923. The *Taunton Courier and Western Advertiser* advertised they would be offering luncheons, teas, light refreshments, grills, *table d'hôte* dinners and a soda fountain. The *table d'hôte* menu was four courses plus coffee and cost 3s 6d. An orchestra consisting of a pianist, cellist, violinist and a vocalist would also perform at set times throughout the day.

Previously the site was that of Tone Bridge House, built and occupied as a family residence for many decades. For a period of time it was used as a factory before

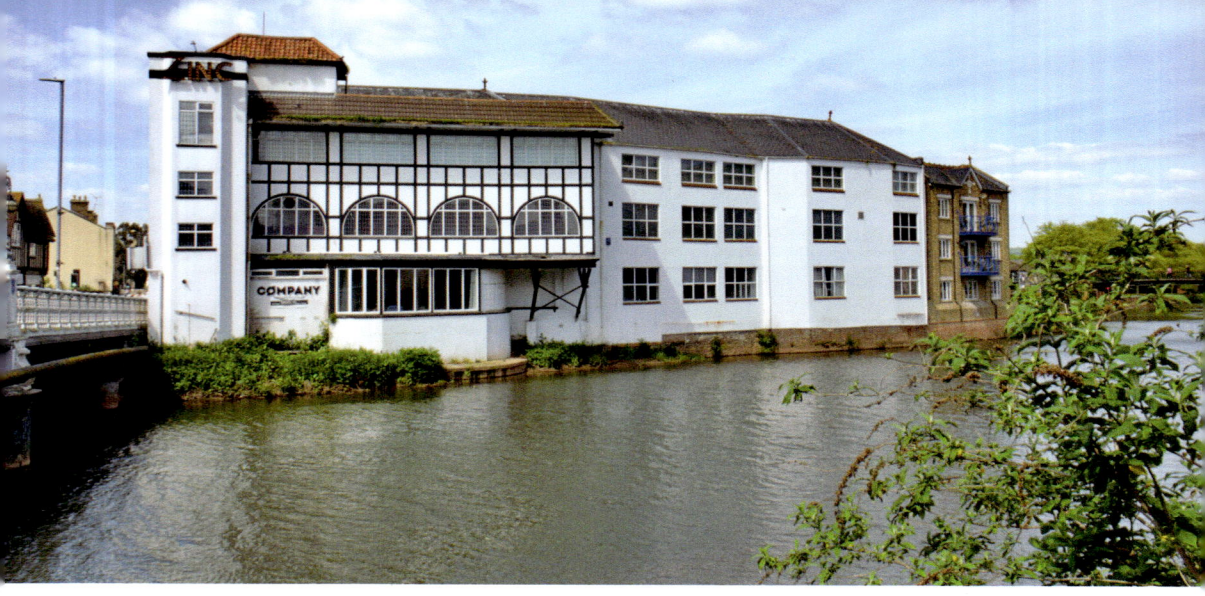

The former Deller's Café, now offices and nightclub 'Zinc'.

being acquired by Deller's and converted through part of 1922/23 into the café. Taunton architects Stone and Lloyd designed the altered building, and works were carried out by Spiller and Browne of Taunton. Some of the internal furnishings were supplied by local firm Hatcher's. The press described the cheerful remodelled exterior: 'looks a typical café with something of a continental touch'.

The ground floor had a shop selling confectionery and cooked meats, and a soda fountain that supplied cold drinks, ice creams and sundaes. A grand central staircase led to the first-floor restaurant and orchestra gallery. The second floor was a separate suite with a supper room and dance floor for private functions. It was quite different in design to the first two floors, being decorated more like an old English barn.

Modern touches included an electric dishwasher, a coffee-roasting room, an electric 'Hobart' potato peeling and cleaning machine and an ice-cream-making room.

Cadena Cafés bought Deller's in February 1933 and in 1956 closed it as it was making a loss. The West Somerset Co-operative Society became the new owners and made alterations to the premises so the ground floor would retail radio and TV amongst other electrical goods. The first floor was to become offices and the hall on the second floor was renamed the Riverside Rooms. There is still a nightclub, Zinc, operating on the top floor.

46. Gaumont Palace, 1932

The Gaumont Palace – later Gaumont Theatre, then Odeon and now Mecca Bingo – is situated on Corporation Street. It was opened on 11 July 1932 by Mayor W. E. Maynard JP and the opening performance was a musical comedy entitled *Sunshine Susie*.

The building was started in August 1931 by a British team with British materials, many of which were sourced locally. The architect was Mr William T. Benslyn of Birmingham and London who reportedly had a great love for the area so was keen to use local materials. The principal building material was Ham Hill stone around a 'steel framed theatre construction'. Lighting was impressive, with thousands of coloured lamps controlled by hand dimmers.

Above the grand entranceway are sculpted panels and a panel depicting *Love and Life Entangled in the Film* by Newbury A. Trent. The ceiling of the auditorium was designed in one piece and described in great detail in the *Taunton Courier* of 6 July 1932. The article also described the 'many wonderful features' of the new cinema, which could seat 1,500 and had the 'best acoustic properties'.

The café was on the first floor and is now office space. Open daily from 11 a.m., it served morning coffee, with lunch, teas and suppers throughout the day up to 10 p.m. By December 1932 seats with specialised apparatus had been installed which allowed those who were deaf to hear by using headphones that were adjustable by means of a simple volume control.

As well as a cinema, the venue was used for live concerts and performances such as those by the Taunton Choral Society and the BBC Orchestra. It has been used as a venue for many live bands including the Beatles. It was renamed the Odeon in 1969 and continued to operate as a cinema until 1981 when it became a bingo hall.

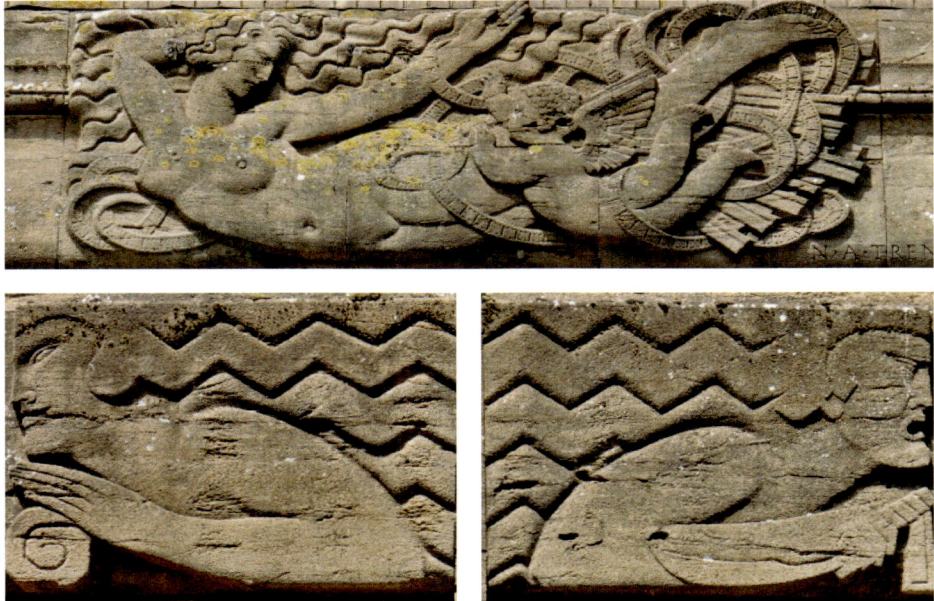

Decorative panels sculpted by Mr A. Hinton and by N. A. Trent.

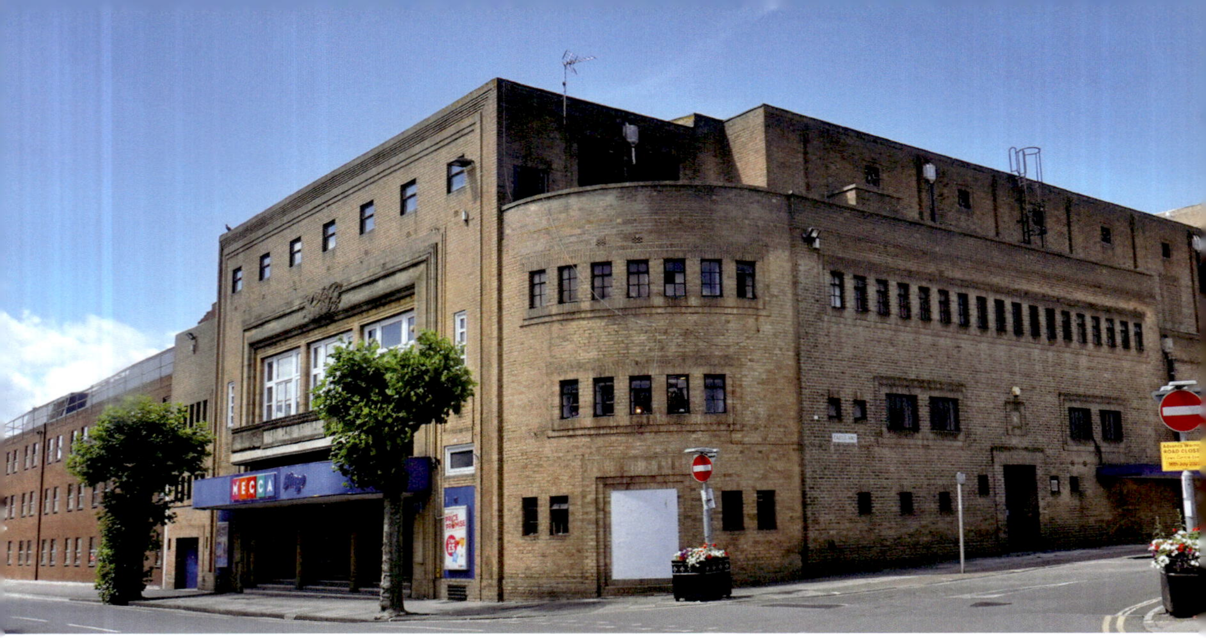

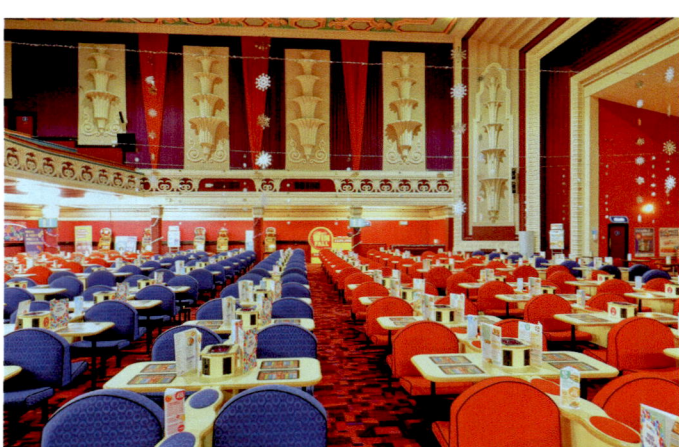

Above: Mecca Bingo and former Gaumont Palace on Corporation Street.

Left: The original interior is vivid: fountain motifs are repeated from the ante proscenium to the balcony. (Used with permission of Mecca)

47. County Hall, 1935

County Hall is situated on The Crescent and was built in 1935 to designs by E. Vincent Harris. Shire Hall on Shuttern had been the home of Somerset County Council since its formation following the Local Government Act of 1888. The council was scattered across various sites within the county and before 1897 had moved to Weston-super-Mare, laying on special trains for the staff commute.

As the work of the council expanded, the need for a purpose-built building was identified. The new County Hall was built of buff and pink brick in a neo-Georgian style. It had two wings, each with eleven bays of sash windows. The entranceway is situated to the centre of a concave building frontage and a tympanum sports a dragon, the county emblem, which was carved in teak by Mr John Hodge.

In August 1935, the various departments began moving into the new premises. The health, education, clerk's and treasurer's departments were moved by 'pantechnicon' from the Weston offices on what became known as the 'Taunton Trail'.

A description of the premises at the opening stated that the building was one of the first in the country of a new type: a purpose-built office building designed for utmost efficiency. The basement provided 4,000 square feet of storage for records. The ground floor plus three upper storeys gave a total of 41,000 square feet of office space. Heating was provided by a 'panel heating' system in which warm water was supplied through pipes embedded in the ceiling. The total cost was £113,500.

By the 1960s further expansion was needed. The first extension was a quadrangle on piloti (ground-level supporting columns) dating to 1962–64,

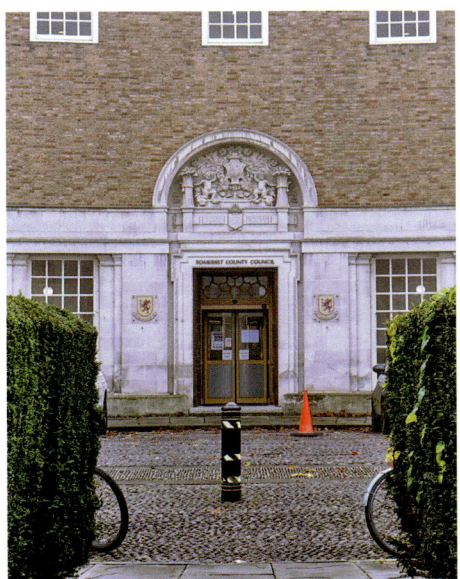

Right: County Hall's entrance, showing the tympanum and the county symbol of a dragon.

Below: County Hall pictured from Corporation Street.

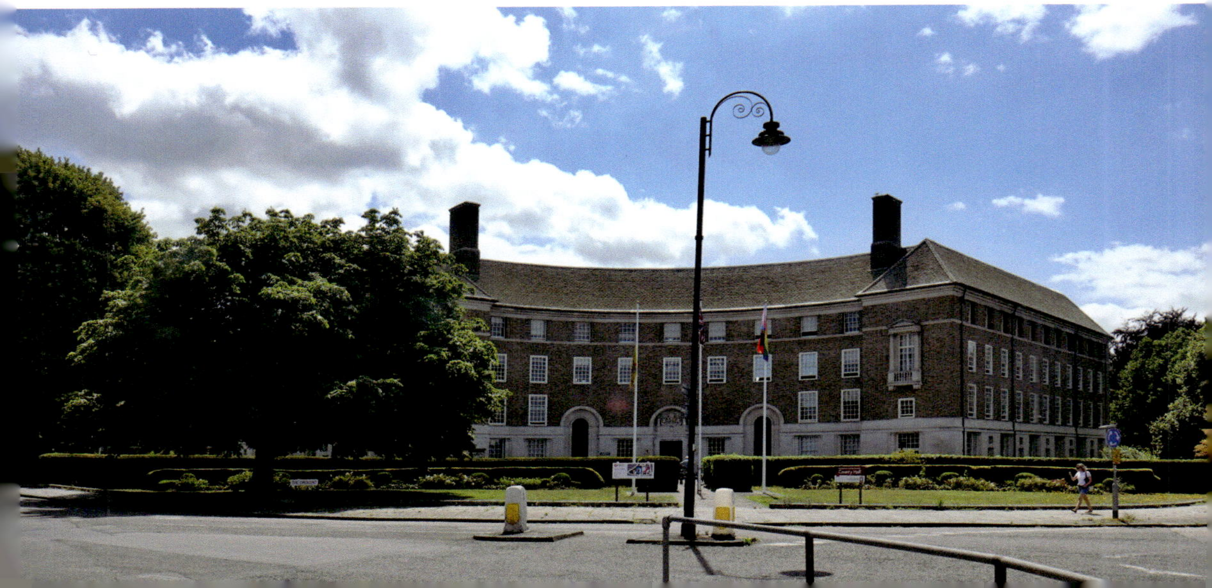

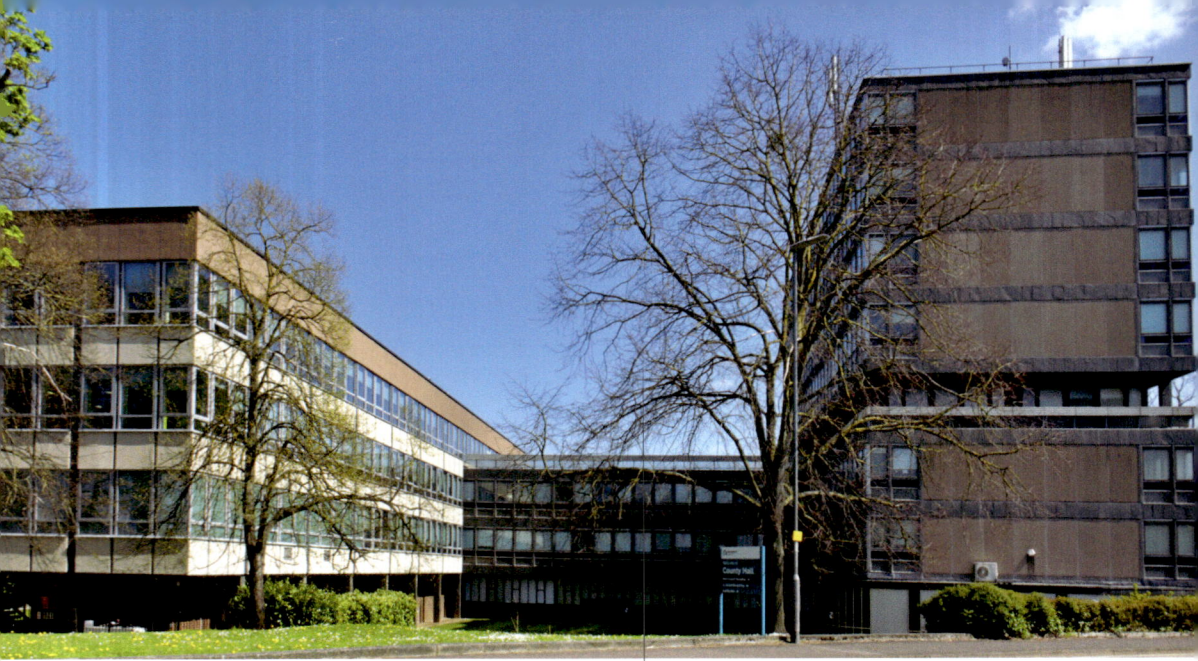

The 1960s additions to County Hall from Shuttern.

and in 1969 a later block was added. These extensions filled land to the west of The Crescent, which in 1807 had originally been designated to not be built upon, keeping the view open for the residents of the newly built houses.

48. Musgrove Park Hospital, 1942

Musgrove Park Hospital is situated off the Wellington Road and when first built was in a relatively undeveloped area of the town. Constructed by the British Army as a military hospital, it was opened in 1942. It was then listed as part of the 'Bolero Building Programme' for US forces in preparation for D-Day under 'hospitals as an expansion' with 1,094 beds. In January 1943, it was occupied by the American Medical Corps until 1946 when it was taken over by the Ministry of Pensions and Somerset County Council.

In 1949, it was suggested that the current hospital on East Reach should be moved to Musgrove when the lease to the Ministry expired as it was bigger and would reduce waiting lists. For a time, of the 450 beds, 120 were reserved for ex-servicemen and the rest for civilians. Somerset County Council ran some maternity beds and other services. From March 1950 departments from East Reach started the transfer across town. All beds, including the military portion, would be under the care of the Taunton Hospital Management Board. This building still houses the operating theatres, critical care and the maternity units, and is one of the oldest NHS buildings in the country, although plans to replace it are described as 'active'.

In 1950, Musgrove became a National Health Service hospital, and it is now run by Somerset NHS Foundation Trust. Over the decades, many expansions and

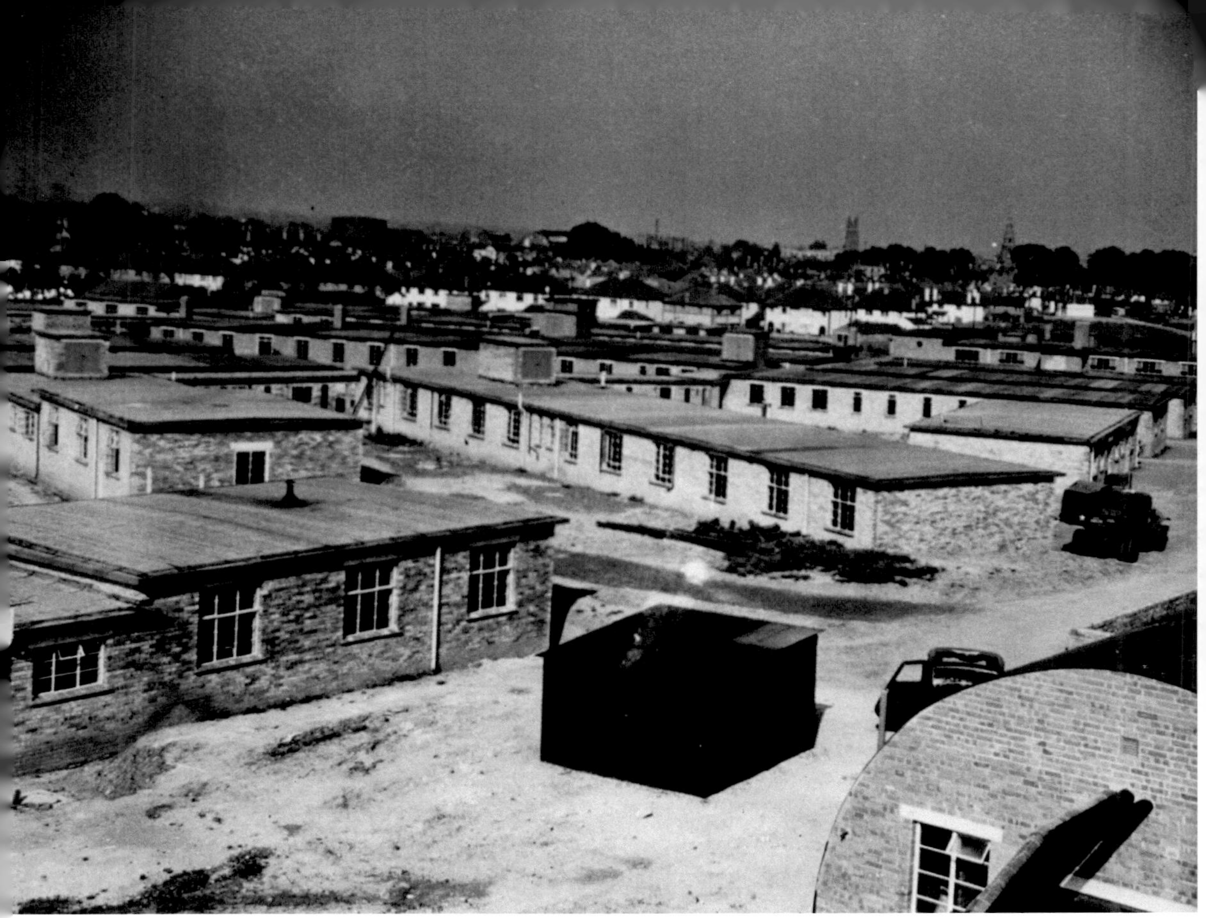

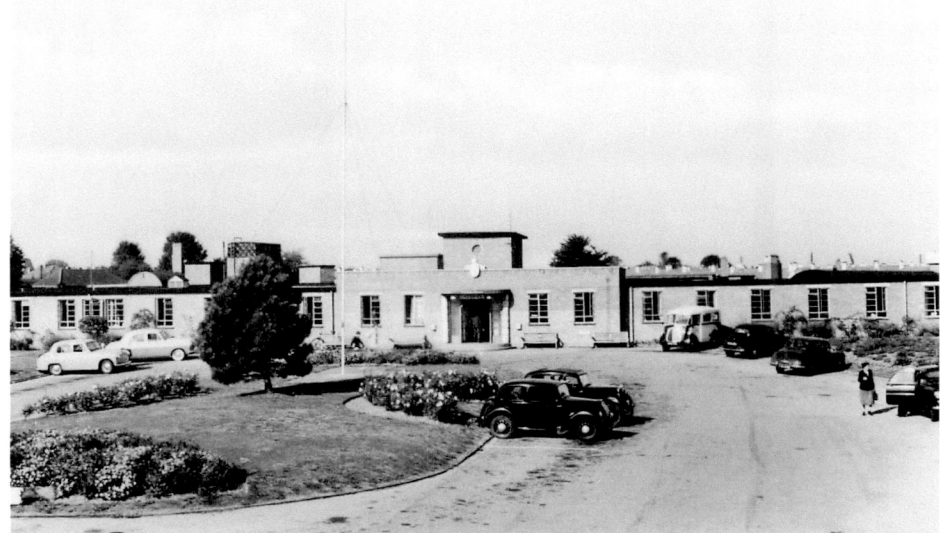

Above: An American image of the newly constructed rows of hospital buildings in 1943.

Below: The original entrance of Musgrove Park Hospital post-1952.

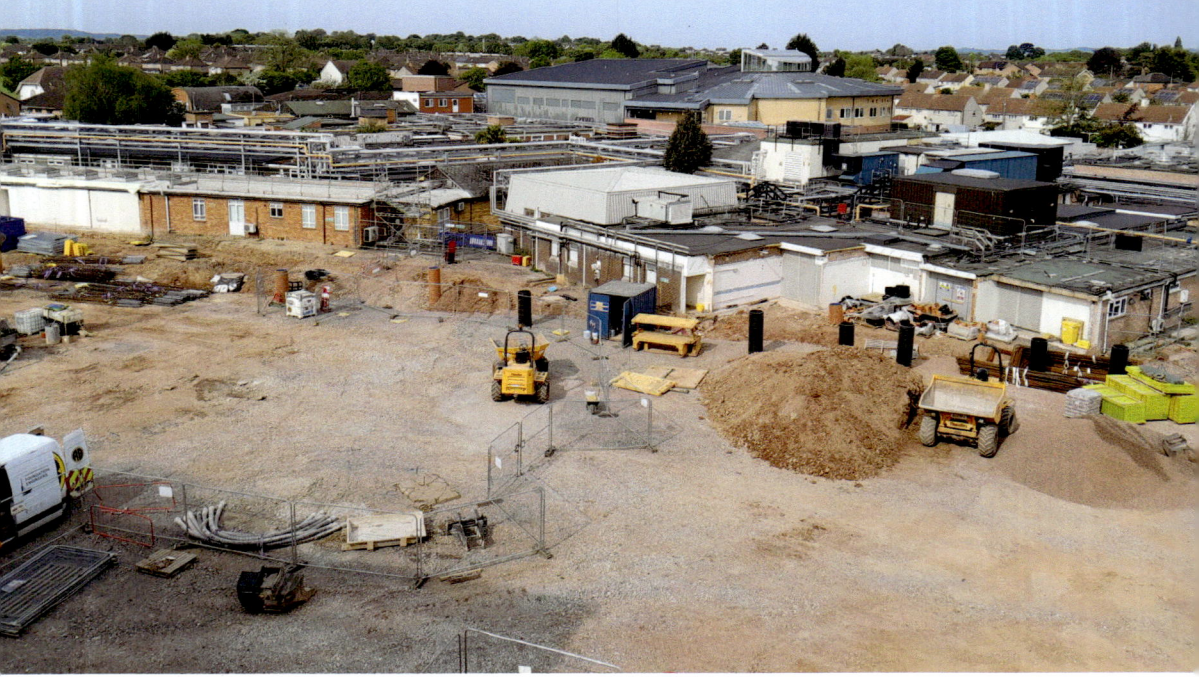

An aerial view of the 2023 development, showing the old brick buildings and the Beacon Centre in the distance. (Courtesy of Kier)

improvements have been made. In 1987, the Queen's Building was opened, the Duchess Building came in 1995, and in 2014 the Jubilee Building. Building work is currently underway for the new surgical centre, which is due to open in 2024 as part of Musgrove 2030, an ambitious programme to transform hospital facilities.

49. Bus Station, 1952

The town's bus station is situated on Tower Street, next to Castle Green, in the centre of town. The new station replaced four bus stops situated around The Parade.

The 'hub' station was built in 1952 and designed by H. A. Starkey for the Western National Omnibus Company. It opened in 1953 with two storeys, the upper jettying out over the ground floor and providing shelter for passengers waiting below. The upstairs offices gave a good view of the bus traffic below, enabling good management. Passenger facilities included a waiting room, toilets, an information centre and a ticket office.

In 2015, the station was awarded a Red Wheel heritage plaque by the Transport Trust, marking the site as 'a rare survivor of a corporate style once common in towns and cities nationwide'. First Bus announced in 2020 that it was going to close the station and there was a public outcry. Some stops were moved back to The Parade, while others were in the vicinity of Castle Way.

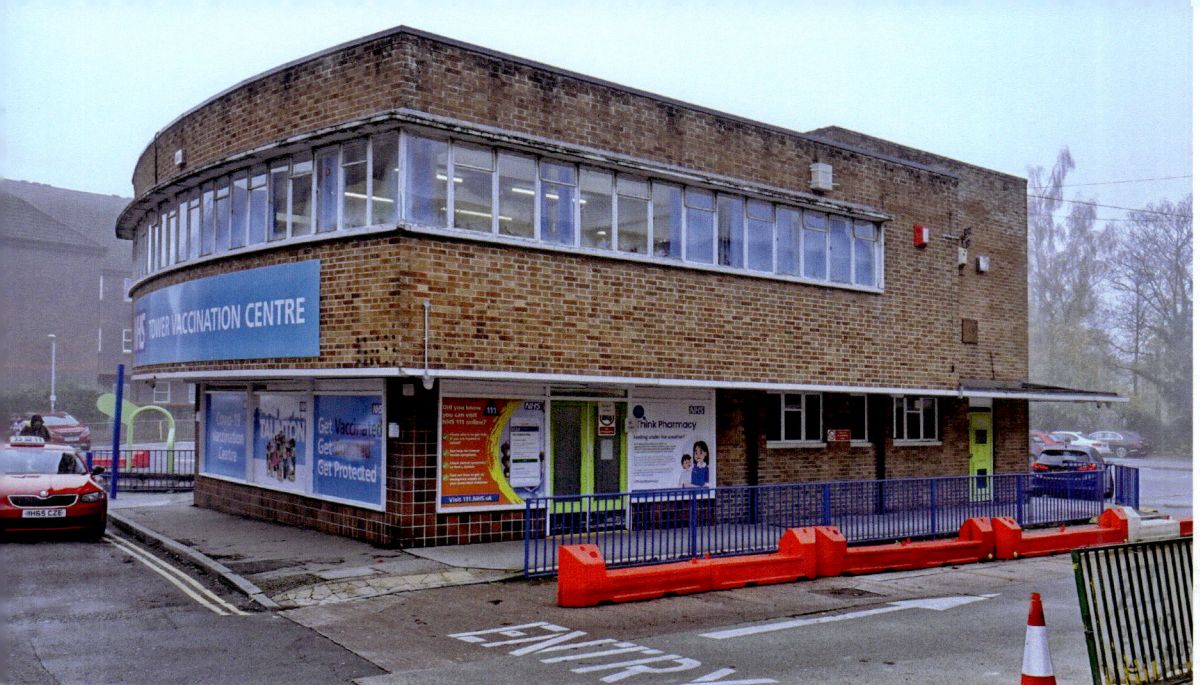

The 1952 bus station while it was in use as a vaccination centre in November 2022.

In May 2023, the station was still being used as a vaccination centre for Covid-19. Early in 2023 discussions regarding Somerset's Bus Service Improvement Plan mooted reopening the bus station, with considerable improvements made possible by government funding.

50. Brewhouse Theatre, 1977

The Brewhouse Theatre is situated by the River Tone and cricket ground and was opened on 28 March 1977 following a thirty-year period of planning. The opening performance was an Alan Ayckbourn favourite: *The Norman Conquests*, starring a little-known David Jason.

Following the Second World War there was a lack of provision for live theatre in the town, with the last suitable venue having been turned over to cinema. A number of enthusiasts formed the Taunton Area Arts Federation, which was to become the driving force behind the future theatre. The plans, drawn up by local architect Norman Branson, were for a 350-seat theatre, a smaller studio, gallery, workshops and ancillaries. Funding was to come by public subscription with the 'A Theatre in a Thousand Days' scheme. Public subscriptions, although initially successful, tailed off and funds had to be obtained from the Arts Council, Somerset County Council, Taunton Borough Council and Westward TV, who specified their donation was for restoration of the listed Georgian Brewer's House, which was on the proposed site. This 1760s house is now linked to the main theatre buildings and provides office space, kitchen and a bar.

The main auditorium is a proscenium arch theatre (this is the arch that separates the stage from the auditorium). The orchestra pit is flexible and, along with the apron (forestage), can be reconfigured to allow the creation of a vomitorium (passage).

During the 2000s there was a difficult time for the theatre when both government and local funding cuts ultimately resulted in its closure in 2013. Taunton Deane Borough Council stepped in and bought the theatre (they already owned the land), which then became run by a newly formed Taunton Theatre Association. The theatre has since gone from strength to strength and offers a range of activities for all ages including workshops, baby and toddler sessions and exhibitions as well as film, theatre and musical events.

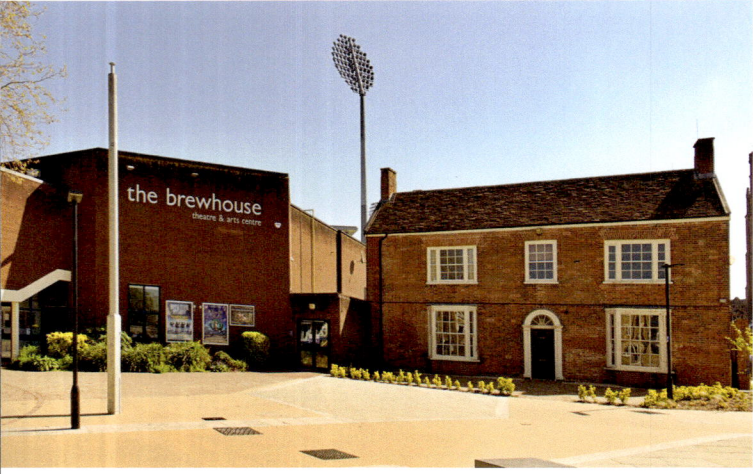

Left: Brewer's House with the theatre to the left.

Below: The Brewhouse complex viewed from St James, showing the 1760 Brewer's House to the left.

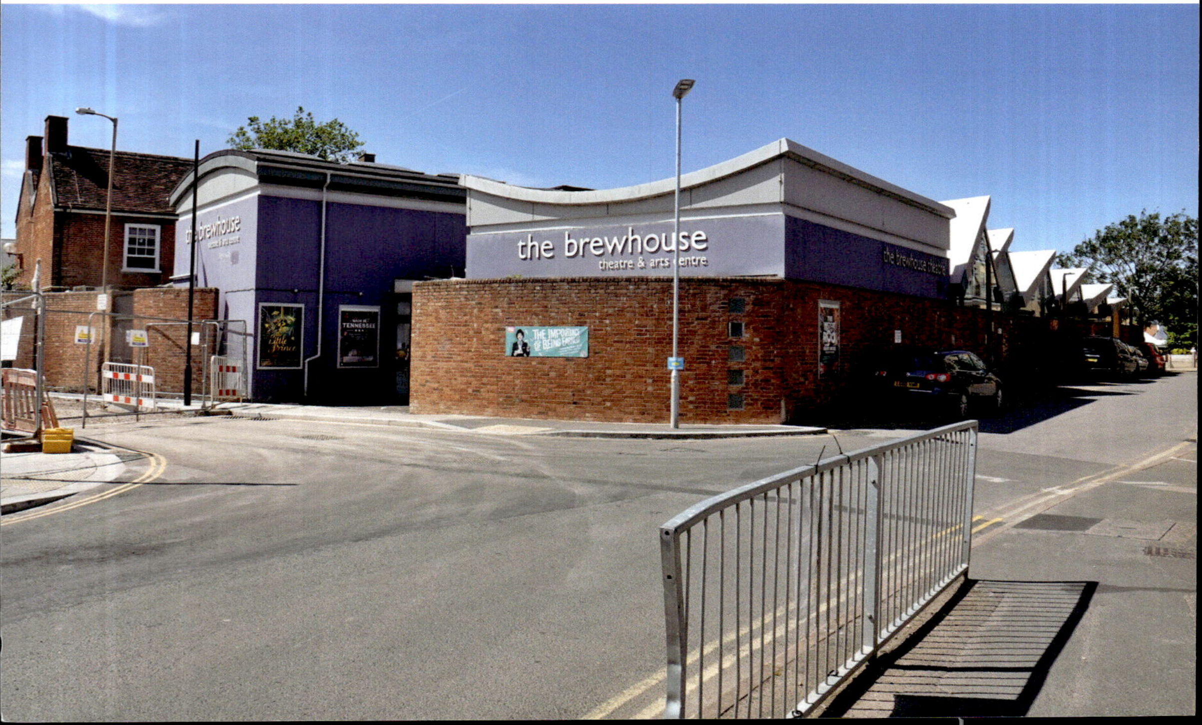

Bibliography

British Newspaper Archive (www.britishnewspaperarchive.co.uk)

Detroit Publishing Co. Ltd (retrieved from the Library of Congress, www.loc.gov/item)

Folkes, J. and C. Bishop, *Taunton: Images of England* (Stroud, Tempus, 2007)

Goldsworthy, E. F., *Recollections of Taunton*, second edition (Taunton, Barnicott & Son, 1883)

Goodman's Guide to Taunton (various years)

Mate's Illustrated Guide to Taunton (1909)

Pevsner, Nikolaus, *Buildings of England: South and West Somerset* (Harmondsworth: Penguin Books Ltd, 1958)

Savage, James, *History of Taunton* (1822 edition, an updated history based on Toumlin's work of 1791)

Somerset Archaeological and Natural History Society publications

Somerset Historic Environment Record (www.somersetheritage.org.uk)

Taunton Trader's Association booklet (1933)

Thomas, Margaret, *A Hero of the Workshop* (1880)

Toumlin, J., *History of Taunton* (1791)

Tuck Postcards Ltd, tuckdbpostcards.org

Where to Buy at Taunton (1893)

Acknowledgements

Thank you to the following for permission to use copyright material in this book: Kier Construction Ltd for supplying an aerial photograph of works at Musgrove Park Hospital; Tom Sherburn, Watchet; and the manager of Mecca Bingo for permission to photograph the interior of the bingo hall in November 2022.

Every attempt has been made to seek permission for copyright material used in this book. However, if we have inadvertently used copyright material without permission/acknowledgement we apologise and we will make the necessary correction at the first opportunity.